30 STRATEGIES for MAKING A FRESH START

STRATEGIES for MAKING A FRESH START

Graham L. Ascough

Published by:

Bas Publishing
ABN 30 106 181 542
ABN 30 106 181 542
PO Box 2052
Seaford Vic 3198
Tel/Fax: (03) 5988 3597

Web: www.baspublishing.com.au
Email: mail@baspublishing.com.au

The National Library of Australia Cataloguing-in-Publication entry

Author: Ascough, Graham L.

Title: 30 strategies for making a fresh start / Graham L. Ascough.

ISBN: 9781921496097 (pbk.)

Subjects: Life skills.
Self-actualization (Psychology)
Change (Psychology)

Dewey Number: 158.1

Design & Layout: Ben Graham

DEDICATION

I wish to dedicate this book to my good friend and mentor

RONA MYERS

For her faith in me, her support and encouragement

and

To all those people who wish to make a fresh start.

Acknowledgements

Many people have participated in the evolution of this book.

I am most grateful for:

My loving wife Carmel, without whose love, encouragement and editorial help this book would not have been written.

My very close friend Rona Myers for her patience, persistence, her astute and penetrating insights. We shared joy and frustration as we played with words and sentences to make the text come alive.

My very good friend Rae Allen for her tremendous support and caring. Over a number of years Rae has seen this book in many different formats and has made some excellent suggestions. Her tenacity has helped to make this book a reality.

Finally, I am very grateful for many of my clients who have trusted their lives with me in counselling and in personal growth groups. Each of you have touched my life in a special way.

Contents

From The Author 9

How To Use This Book. 11

Section 1

SUCCESSFUL LIVING

Strategy 1 At a Crossroad – Finding A Better Way 17

Strategy 2 Changing Direction – Making a Fresh Start 27

Strategy 3 Reinventing Yourself – Daring to Be Different 39

Strategy 4 How To Build Self Confidence and Self Esteem . . . 49

Strategy 5 Believe In Your Uniqueness 59

Strategy 6 Positive Optimism – Believe The Best Is Yet To Be. . 69

Strategy 7 Stop Procrastinating – Make Good Decisions 79

Strategy 8 Waking Up To Life – Life is For Living 89

Strategy 9 Success and Personal Motivation – Setting Realistic Goals 99

Strategy 10 Positive Possibilities - Time to Review Your Progress 109

Section 2

SUCCESSFUL RELATIONSHIPS

Strategy 11 Positive Stress Management– Finding Peace Within. 117

Strategy 12 How to Win Friends – Building Friendships 129

Strategy 13 Creative Communication – Listen, Reflect, Act. . . 139

Strategy 14 Qualities That Attract – Desirable Qualities 149

Strategy 15 Breaking Out Of Your Emotional Prison 159

Strategy 16 Innovative Insights For Living & Relating 169

Strategy 17 Forgiving And Forgetting – Letting Go Of The Past 181

Strategy 18 Steps To Lasting Happiness 191

Strategy 19 How to Play the Game of Life and Win 199

Strategy 20 Follow Head and Heart - Review Your Progress . . . 209

Section 3

SUCCESSFUL LOVING

Strategy 21 Exploring Intimacy – Building Togetherness 219

Strategy 22 Let Us Talk About Love – Straight From The Heart 227

Strategy 23 Love and Actions Go Together 235

Strategy 24 Romance - A Way Adults Play 243

Strategy 25 Sensuality – Touch, Tenderness, Body Image 253

Strategy 26 Rethinking Sexuality – New Discoveries 263

Section 4

SUCCESSFUL NEW BEGINNINGS

Strategy 27 Give Life Everything You Have 277

Strategy 28 It Is Never Too Late to Begin Again. 287

Strategy 29 Change and the New You. 293

Strategy 30 Graduation Day – Making a Fresh Start 299

From The Author

This book *30 Strategies for Making a Frest Start* is one of the most exciting books that I have written. I have gained so much from the book that has enriched my life and spurred me on to the next stage of my fascinating journey.

I can assure you with full participation and openness you will discover new insights, be motivated and learn all about creating the life you have always wanted. Theory has been kept to a basic minimum.

Every strategy I have used in this book I have applied with thousands of clients at the North Shore Counselling and Personal Growth Centre in Sydney where I was Director for 25 years. In all there are 30 strategies which I share and I trust they will work well for you as they have for me.

I believe this book is very timely as we are living in a very insecure world where it has become tough to survive.

My purpose in writing this book is to encourage those who wish to make a fresh start in life. You may even find at this time you have hit rock bottom and do not know what to do next. This book will help you at the critical time in your life. Never, never give up; see this book as a lifeline of hope.

30 Strategies for Making a Frest Start comes out with a wealth of knowledge and experience and backed by 81 years of learning and discovering what living is all about. It comes with a lot of wisdom and insights.

At this time in life I am a Practical Psychology Writer, Life Enrichment Lecturer for Cruise Line P&O, have published three books *Oh Happy, Happy Days: New Rules of Retirement*, *Beginner's Guide To Writing Your Life Story*, and *New Beginnings: A Purpose Driven Life*. I have two more books waiting to be published.

As you study this book and read the case histories of many clients, my wish is that you will be inspired and believe the best of life is yet to be. This is my motto that inspires me and I hope will inspire you.

— Graham Ascough

How To Use This Book

Section 1 – Successful Living

How you think and feel shapes your life. Discover what you want and how to achieve the best result. Know it is time to overhaul your life and make some changes. Learn how to recover from life's cruel blows,

Section 2 – Successful Relationships

Be prepared to face challenges and not run away from them by blaming someone else. Learn about close encounters of the human kind. Market yourself in today's world – believe you deserve joy and happiness.

Section 3 – Successful Loving

Everybody is sexual and needs love and acceptance. Sexuality is a journey from birth to death. There is still much ignorance about sexuality. Rethink love, romance, intimacy, sex.

Section 4 - Successful Frest Start

Now is the time to make a fresh start with new innovative and exciting strategies. Take charge of your life right now! Dare to live the life you have always dreamed about.

Trust and believe in yourself – great men and women have always done so. To know yourself, understand yourself, is to begin to trust yourself. You are now equipped to act upon your thoughts and go forward into a world of spontaneity and challenge. Midlife is a time for rebirth.

Be Your Own Life Coach

Decide on five goals you wish to achieve before you finish this book. All the way through you are responsible for and can change these goals at any time. Without goals there is no clear cut direction. Give yourself permission to experiment with new options.

Personal Reflections

In order to protect your privacy as you record your personal reflections I suggest you buy a journal or a notebook. This is so important if you and your partner are sharing the book. Share with one another when you complete each section. Be as honest as you can in each of the reflections.

Life Coaching Strategies

These are thoughts and ideas to consider in applying the strategies to your current situation.

Notes to Myself

These are found at the end of each Section. They are there for you to jot down thoughts and ideas to reflect upon.

Repetition

Repetition of material is used as an educational tool for reinforced learning.

Seek Professional Guidance

If after completing this book, you feel you need some professional help, check the resources available in your community, or talk to your doctor for a referral.

Section 1

SUCCESSFUL LIVING

At a Crossroad

Changing Direction

Reinventing Yourself

Self Confidence, Self Esteem

You Are Unique

Positive Optimism

Stop Procrastinating

Waking Up To Life

Success And Personal Motivation

Positive Possibilities

STRATEGY 1

At a Crossroad – Finding A Better Way

Stop Postponing the Rest of Your Life

Do you at times have a sense of being in a dark hole with no way out? Do you feel that everything you do goes wrong, with one problem after another and the more you try to solve your problems the more complex they become? Do you feel you are just existing and not really living? Perhaps you are experiencing a marriage breakup, a nervous breakdown, the death of a loved one, loss of a job, a financial crisis, a life threatening disease, an intense sense of loneliness, alienation, depression or some other emotional disappointment. If you are facing any of these crises be rest assured that this book is designed for you – those who wish to make a fresh start.

Life is yours to enjoy. Overcome any negativity or inactivity caused by fear, worry and anxiety. Now is the time to gain a ray of hope as you discover practical approaches to problem solving based on sound common sense.

Be Your Own Life Coach

You know yourself better than anyone else. As you progress through this book you will be encouraged to take control of your life. Suggestions will be made for you to consider but the ultimate decision remains with you. Everyone is different and you need to decide the best approach for you. As you learn to tap into your inner strength, you will decide what is right for you.

Every exercise that you do as you read is important. You cannot fail if you see every experience as a learning experience. Mistakes are not a disgrace but part of a learning process. He who never fails, never does much. Do not be held back by the past. Whatever your age, believe you are ready to make some changes in your life. Dedicate yourself to be the best life coach you can be as you learn to make things happen. You will not be disappointed.

Time To Get Your Life Back On Track

At the present time you may feel that your life is out of control. If you see your problem related to drugs, using alcohol to excess, in the middle of a messy divorce, have a gambling problem, full of lies and deceit but still not accepting responsibility for your actions. Most people have had unpleasant memories of experiences that did not go to plan, or that you felt were out of your control, some people even tend to suppress problems and hope they will go away. But this never happens. If you wish to turn your life around the first step is to take personal responsibility for your choices. We are all accountable for our choices and by taking appropriate action you will know how to cope with personal challenges. Let go of cop outs, excuses, justifications such as "Other people make me act in this way".

Even when life feels really tough try never to lose sight of your sense of humour and fun, as it can be a temporary relief from your problems. Believe you are resilient and able to bounce back from setbacks.

To turn your life around you need to do something. No one can actually force you to change; the decision to turn your life around must come from within. Resolve now to do whatever it takes and to learn that living is far better than just surviving. Be true to your real self, show a willingness to live in the present moment with some new skills and become a free spirit.

Let Challenges Make You Stronger

Life can seem to be running along smoothly but suddenly you are challenged and the bottom falls out of your world. Everything that was nice and easy now looks bleak and dismal. This can happen unexpectedly and often appears not to be of your making. At times like these you need to draw upon your inner strength and roll with the punches in order to bounce back. In spite of the setbacks stay positive and keep moving forward. Learn to discern the true nature of a situation, experiment with ways of overcoming a problem and treat it as a way to grow. Do not be bound by the "shoulds and oughts". Plot your new course of action by being true to yourself. It may seem to some to be a selfish action but realise at times such actions are necessary.

Life is a series of lessons and each one comes in the form of a challenge. Ask yourself "What is life trying to teach me in this experience?" This helps you to turn a challenge into a learning experience. When you learn one of life's lessons you move on. Slow down and take time to see what life is teaching you.

Life Is Full Of Choices and Adjustments

At life's crossroads you are not always sure which way to go. You need to reflect on all aspects of life before you make a decision. A crossroad can produce pain and anxiety. Sometimes it is in the form of a 'speed bump' to slow you down or a 'traffic calming device' to question whether or not you are on the right track. Discomfort is often a part of this learning experience. The aim is to break free of bad habits that hold you back – visualize yourself succeeding and there will be less discomfort.

Mistakes are easy to make when you feel confused. Listen to others and be open to suggestions they make, but give them a lot of thought before making your own decision. Look carefully at yourself and get a clear understanding of what you need to change in your life to progress.

The right decision will evolve at the right time so never make a choice out of desperation, fear and confusion. An inner knowing will assist you in making the right choice.

Time To Break Out Of A Mould

Breaking out of a mould takes strength and courage. Stop playing the pretending game. If something is not working in your life you need to step out of your comfort zone and do something about it. Yes, there can be some pain and confusion involved; in gaining any new skills you may feel awkward but be consistent and persevere. Do not look for the easy way out or drift back into your old pattern which caused the problem. Explore skills which enhance your life. Focus on what is working as your life is your creation.

When Things Go Wrong – Do Not Quit

Failure is a natural part of being human, but let the words of Winston Churchill ring true for you today, "Never, never, never give up". Whenever you feel fearful or doubtful about anything that you want to attempt say enthusiastically to yourself, "I can and I will, I can and I will, I can and I will!" When you start saying, "I can do it, I can do it," you drive that message deep into your subconscious mind. This message lowers your fears and builds your self confidence. The pain of life's problems may seem unbearable but be true to your own convictions. You know what works for you. Hold on to your beliefs and discard the rest. Once you accept your human imperfections you realise you can rectify some of your mistakes and move ahead. In tough times new lessons are learned so do not keep punishing yourself but learn from the past and move on.

Ask yourself "Why have these problems come about?" Accept personal responsibility. There are some problems that come your way which are out of your control – bush fire, accident and natural disasters etc, but when these disasters come your way see what you can learn.

Divide your problem into manageable portions and set realistic goals in handling them. If the problem persists, you may need to seek professional help. This is not a sign of weakness. Counselling helps a person to gain a clear understanding of a complex situation and can offer valuable insights towards a solution.

Re-examine Core Values and Beliefs

You learn values from your parents and other authority figures. Many basic beliefs from childhood remain constant. However, the world has changed and you may need to find your own set of values. What worked for your parents may not necessarily work for you today. Approach your belief system with an open mind and be very honest with yourself. Examine what could be regarded as a rigid thought patterns. With age, maturity and new knowledge you need to determine what to hold on to and what to discard. See new patterns of belief emerging which could be worth exploring. Nourish and assimilate new information as there is always more to learn about yourself and life. Give positive acknowledgement to these new thoughts.

Moving Beyond Powerlessness

In some difficult situations you can feel powerless. It can be a horrible feeling of helplessness and even hopelessness. Everything seems blocked and you feel as if you are paralysed and dissatisfied with your life. You are ready for change.

In moments of desperation it is wise to stop and give yourself time to find strength, regroup your thoughts, devise a plan of action and then slowly move forward. Being patient like this helps you to move from powerlessness to a feeling that you are in control of a situation. Do not regret the past as it has something to teach you, let the future take care of itself. Live only in the present and do one thing at a time to move from powerlessness to action.

Believe the answers to life's problems are within you. Draw upon this power and take time to search within to know what is right. Remember anyone can make a mistake. Make a contract with yourself and be determined to find a better way.

Rethinking the Way You Live

Being at a crossroad helps you to rethink what you want from life. Life is what you make it so strive for something better. Recognise that you are fed up with your old ways of doing things and explore different pathways. Interpret events positively by looking for the best outcome.

Along the way there will be challenges and some difficult decisions as you seek a solution to inner emptiness. Listen to the thoughts that you are feeling as there may be a fear of change or some confusion about coping with a new life. Acknowledge these thoughts and look at how you might overcome them. Be open to the belief that there could be a better way to live that will bring you a sense of joy, peace or happiness. Cultivate a sense of adventure and curiosity in your life.

Discovering a Better Way

As you complete strategy number one be excited about the future. Be aware that for a long time the universe may have been nudging you to do "something" and now you have taken your first step. An ancient Chinese proverb says "If you do not change the direction you are going, you are likely to end up where you are heading". This is a sobering thought. Take action and make some changes.

Finding a better way means having a willingness to experiment with new ways of living. Let go of the excuses and justifying behaviour, explore new ideas. Be accountable for the decisions you make. Recognise inspirational moments when thoughts expressed fit perfectly into your situation.

Believe within, you have enormous reserves of capability, potential, and talent that you haven't come close to using. These reserves lay deep within you, a goldmine of human resources waiting to be released and put to use in your life. Be prepared to explore and experiment while discovering a better way of living and relating.

Personal Reflection

1. Describe a crossroad you find yourself at this time.

   . . . .

   . . . .

   . . . .

   . . . .

   . . . .

2. Decide any positive steps you might take to turn your life in a positive direction.

   Step One: . . . .

   . . . .

   Step Two: . . . .

   . . . .

   Step Three: . . . .

   . . . .

   Step Four: . . . .

   . . . .

3. Write down your immediate action plan:

   . . . .

   . . . .

   . . . .

   . . . .

   . . . .

   . . . .

Action Strategies

Engage in positive self-talk. Be your own cheerleader.

Believe in what you can become – believe in yourself and your ability to grow through this situation.

See a crossroad as an opportunity for growth – and every experience, however tough as an opportunity to transform you into a better person.

Choose your reaction – rise above a victim mentality.

Activate your mind – find the best possible solution based on information available.

Recognise old patterns that no longer work in your life, and be prepared to replace them with new ones that work.

STRATEGY 2

Changing Direction – Making a Fresh Start

If You Are Unhappy Do Something About It

You know whether you are happy or not. Many of us go through life playing a pretending game consciously (and sometimes unconsciously) living a lie. Be one of those authentic persons who know what they want from life and do all you can to achieve your goals. Admit you are willing to make some changes. No matter how things are you still have a choice however limited it may seem.

Taking Stock, Taking Aim, Taking a New Direction

This kind of thinking helps you to take stock of what is important to you and what is unimportant. Life can be so busy that you get carried away with things that consume your time and energies but are not truly satisfying. You may feel reasonably happy but you know there is still something missing. Taking stock causes you to reflect and prioritise. Instead of having a life crammed full of activities, have a balanced approach to life by choosing when to be active or to be still and reflective. Go within and find what it is that drives you to achieve your goals, and develop a sense of knowing when you need to be still. Accept the fact that 'this' moment has a message for you.

Taking aim means identifying things that you enjoy doing. As you take aim you have a far better chance to hit the bullseye as you have a new point of focus. You then put your energy into things that are meaningful in life and bring satisfaction. Be prepared to let go of concepts that no longer serve you in reaching your ultimate goals. Decide what really matters to you. When you do this there could be a shift in values.

A label is a liability especially if it has a negative connotation. Some labels such as those given to you by a family member, a teacher, or friends etc stick even when you know deep down it is not true. It is possible to free yourself from these labels and make life work for you. Reassure yourself that change is right for you at this time.

No Time Is Ever Perfect For Major Changes

There is never a perfect time for change, major or minor. But when you recognize you are having difficulties you know that you need to do something. If you see it necessary to change your work, your lifestyle, your relationship or your beliefs, there will always be reasons and excuses that indicate this is not the right time. Do not wait until you see your health being affected and forced to make a decision.

When your decision to change affects other people they need to know your reasons. Take personal responsibility for your actions and have reasons clearly thought out. Nothing is ever achieved by blaming others. Resolve in your mind to make appropriate changes. Even the smallest attempt can make a world of difference. Value the process of change and recognize that you have something worthwhile to contribute to life.

Take The Initiative

Opportunities sometimes come your way and you fail to recognise them. When someone else takes the initiative and seizes that opportunity you could feel regretful about what you missed. Believe you have the ability to act differently and make decisions about change in your life as you break free from the past and initiate a plan or strategy to deal with a particular problem.

Taking the initiative without doing your homework can prove to be a costly mistake. Fully investigate an opportunity before taking action. Acting on the spur of the moment is a pathway to disaster. Take time to assess every situation and be responsible for all your actions.

If communication in a relationship breaks down one partner can take the initiative and address the issue. Be sure the focus is on the relationship problem not upon personalities. If this action is taken the initiator has to accept the consequences of the action. Be open to meaningful communication. Let the other person know you have listened without interruption. Listen first and then discuss the issue.

Facing the Challenge of Change

Change is a part of life but on the whole we find it difficult. We fear the uncertainty of change. Some may see change as a threat to their security. If you feel you want to improve your self esteem and develop your potential you have no option but to change. Learn to live with it. Be prepared to invent new ways of doing things. Be open to all that life presents.

In a relationship there can be problems when one person wishes to grow and experiment with life and the other sees these actions as a threat. The issue must be discussed with open minds when differing points of view are expressed. Listen to one another. Respect one another's opinions.

Keep growing, expanding and reaching for the best life has to offer you. Do not accept second best. Assess now what is happening and reward yourself for trying, not simply in what you actually accomplish. Believe the best day of your life is today – make the most of it. See your life as an incredible gift and let life challenge you with a new vision. Be a refreshing agent of change.

Know Who You Are and Where You Want to Go

Take time to catch up with yourself and really discover who you are and what you want from life. How you perceive yourself determines how you portray yourself. It is human nature to want to be like someone else. Look for qualities you admire in people but at the same time search to find who you are and develop your self esteem and self worth in a manner acceptable to you. In creating a better you, design yourself around your needs, priorities, values, and talents. Be honest with yourself and know that in acknowledging the areas that need change takes courage.

How do you fit into the world? What character traits do you value? What qualities are contained in your unique and special personality? Knowing your character can help you understand areas for change. Do not feel you have to follow others. People have different personalities, and this diversity is what makes life interesting.

Take time to record your interests, hobbies, talents, and gifts. What or who has influenced you? What are your accomplishments? How do you manage adversity? How do you handle relationships? What really makes you happy?

Now you can begin to create the person you want to be. Take any of your negative thoughts about yourself and rethink them in a positive way. For example, instead of thinking of yourself as a victim, think as a survivor. Remember; change your perspective and your reality changes. You will see life differently.

Be open to new ideas and see where they will take you. You need to take time to put yourself together and be comfortable with changes you are making in your life, before making a change in your career. It is not a career which will help you feel good about yourself but your willingness to accept personal responsibility for who you have become. Know what you crave for and distinguish new emerging patterns that nourish your life and help you find direction.

Once you have decided where you want to be in the next five years be prepared to work out a plan to achieve this goal. Never sell yourself short. Value who you are and feel confident about the contribution you can make to enrich the lives of those who are closest to you. Become aware of how you affect others around you. Be generous with encouraging comments.

All this helps to make change very worthwhile as everyone benefits. Share your dream with important people in your life and enlist their support. Drop your defences and value the feedback. Be open to fresh insights.

Ask Yourself "What Do I Need to Learn?"

For most of us this is not an easy question to face as we often run away from lessons we need to learn. Learning from our mistakes is a key to resolving problems and creating a better life. It is important not to look negatively at any mistakes from the past because these help us to grow. Identify any negative thought patterns that appear to be entrenched in your mind that hinders progress. Have these been the cause of some your problems? Take a stand and turn these around by making them into positive statements. Talk to yourself positively all of the time.

Life is a school and it is not until you learn each lesson well do you move on to the next lesson. Stubborn people who fail to admit they are wrong stumble through life. They are their own worst enemy. Recognise what you need to learn to make life better for yourself and others.

Expand Your Thinking

Expand your thinking and continue to feed your mind with positive thoughts. Replace "that's the way it is", with "I can do better". You can do something. Be open to new ideas. Try to reach out and look at new ideas. Follow up thoughts with actions. Monitor your performance as you expand your thinking. Turn a thought or idea into a belief and act upon it. Nothing has real meaning except the meaning you give it

Personal Liberation

Changing direction can be a form of personal liberation. Focus on your true self not what others expect you to be. It is truly a liberating feeling when you come to a stage in life when you are free to be yourself. Make your life more enjoyable by doing things you really enjoy but have not done for some time.

It is a time for people to love you "warts and all", you also need to accept others as they are. Perhaps at this point you need to see your children as equals and be friends. This can only happen if there is a deep sense of mutual self respect. Re-evaluate family relationships and make changes you deem necessary. Adopt a flexible attitude – one of equality.

Have the strength of your convictions to go ahead and make the changes that you feel are desirable. Things around you are changing all the time. In fact you may feel flat out keeping up with your changing world.

Be Free to Be You

Being yourself helps you to live out your unexpressed side. Maybe you wish to be less serious and express more fun. Perhaps you need to laugh more and cry less? Maybe you dislike your conservative approach to life and wish to be more of a risk taker? There could be a rebellion going on inside you and that you are angry about the way life and work has changed you. You may have felt that you have lost your way? You may even feel that you are living a lie and no-one really knows you. Be prepared now to share truths that you hold dear. Listen to your heart and think with your head.

Building on Your Achievements

Reflect on what you have already achieved. We have all achieved something in our lives. What have you achieved? Why did it work? What personal skills helped you achieve it? Skills are building blocks to success and achievement. Identify your skills – personal, academic, work, etc. Focus on how you can use these skills and past achievements to help you make changes in the present. What is it you want to change?

Learn to use what you have, to get what you want. Recognise your gifts, talents, and skills. Analyse carefully if you are happy in what you do or whether it may be time for a major change. Think carefully before you make a change. Give yourself something to look forward to. Break free of rigid patterns that no longer work.

Accept Life Has Uneasiness

As I have said before there will be times when you feel uneasy, perhaps even out of your depth, and you will be struggling as you try to cope. It is during these times you learn much about yourself and your life, the greater the crisis the greater the opportunity for you to learn more. Do what it takes to overcome your uneasiness. Learn new skills. Talk to people. Be committed to extending your horizons – be unstoppable. Take into consideration those around you and how you affect them. Recognise if you are out of your depth and respond to the challenge. Talk to a counsellor, or a friend, but above all remain positive.

Endings and Beginnings

See every ending as a new beginning filled with possibilities. This could be the ending of a relationship, a job, retirement, death of a loved one, children leaving home, a serious illness and other issues which cause you to make some adjustments. When something ends in your life ask yourself "What did I learn?"

When marriage ends in divorce, many feel it is the end of the road. After you recover from the initial shock of the event and understand the reasons for the breakup you need to regroup your inner resources and see the way forward to a new beginning. Basically we are all creatures of habit and do not like to be disturbed. Sometimes a severe shake up will take you out of a world of complacency, and forced in a new direction not sure where it will go.

A new beginning at first may be a fearful experience but as the momentum increases and confidence is established, life emerges differently. You experience a new lease of life and a situation that looked so hopeless now has renewed energy and a clear cut direction. Progress is usually made with small steps, however, everybody is different proceed with caution.

No Time for Complacency –Be Committed

No one knows how much time anyone, young or old, has left. Do not be complacent and let life drift along aimlessly. Take some positive action. Find something that you really want to do, and look at how you can achieve it. Decide on a course of action to have your needs met. Face any or all of your fears.

Henry Newman said "Fear not that your life will come to an end, but rather that it shall never have a beginning". Heed this warning. Become the best person you can possibly be. Making life a fulfilling, exhilarating experience is dependent on the amount of diligence and effort you put into the situation.

Be Excited About Possible Outcomes

As you discover new approaches in living, based on commonsense, perhaps you may even be surprised that you did not think of the idea earlier, develop an attitude of gratitude for what you are discovering about yourself and life.

Make each day a new day for learning about life. Approach it with high anticipation and become excited with the prospects and possible outcome. Put problems into their proper perspective and start to think and talk positively.

Case Study

Ron's Story

Ron's mother was a school principal and always wanted her three boys to be teachers. Ron's mother saw the importance of education and felt teaching was a safe job. Ron's father had died at an early age. The family struggled for survival. Ron always felt shy and insecure, but he was a bright student and loved mathematics.

At the end of high school Ron followed his mother's suggestion and enrolled in a teacher training course. His heart was not in the study program. At the end of the first year he just scraped through. Halfway through second year Ron became ill and was admitted to hospital with a mystery illness. He lost weight, suffered severe headaches and became seriously depressed and was sent to visit a psychiatrist. After a few weeks he was discharged from hospital and was told he would be ready to go back to teacher training college within a couple of weeks. Three days prior to going back to college Ron became ill again. A friend suggested that Ron might like to talk to a counsellor.

He agreed to come to counselling. He talked much about home, family and his mother. He told me how much he idolised his mother and would do nothing to hurt her. I asked for permission to see his mother. His mother agreed to come as she wanted to make sure I knew “all the facts”. She insisted that she knew what was right for Ron. The mother talked incessantly until I started to ask her questions about herself. At first she was defensive, but as I gained her respect she opened up. We discussed Ron’s unhappiness, his health problems, his relationship with her and about what she believed was best for her boys. The two other boys were at Teachers College and were doing very well.

I suggested to the mother there could be a conflict in Ron’s mind about what he wanted to do and what she wanted him to do. At first the mother was hostile about this thought but agreed to go home and think about it.

That night she and Ron had their most meaningful discussion in years. Ron was open with his mother and she listened intently. At last she accepted the fact that Ron was old enough to make up his own mind. By the next morning Ron had made up his mind to leave the course. Almost overnight his health improved. Within two weeks he had a job.

Ron had a part time job whilst he made up his mind. He decided on an arts commerce course at Sydney University and hopes to do the Master of Business Administration. He is now in his second year and gained some distinctions. His health is excellent. He is a new person as he heads in the direction of his choice.

Personal Reflections

1. Pin point an area of your life you would like to change. Indicate reasons why you are unhappy.

. . . .

. . . .

. . . .

. . . .

. . . .

2. What do you believe it is that stops you from making some changes in your life? What are you going to do about the situation?

. . . .

. . . .

. . . .

. . . .

. . . .

3 To achieve the changes you wish to make decide on a course of action. Insert a date for competition of each change you wish to make.

. . . .

. . . .

. . . .

. . . .

. . . .

. . . .

Action Strategies

One door closes another opens – become an opportunity spotter.

Give yourself permission to change your direction – pathway to freedom and personal liberation.

Build bridges, not walls – take down your walls and move forward.

Break out of your mould – have courage to admit you are on the wrong track. Do something about it.

Turn mistakes into stepping stones – learn from your mistakes and move on.

Listen to the inner self – this tells you that you are on the right track.

Adjust your focus – some minor changes can make all the difference.

Stand by your convictions – you know what is right for you.

STRATEGY 3

Reinventing Yourself – Daring to Be Different

Learning To Reinvent Yourself – Upgrading Your Identity

Personal identity is the way you see or define yourself; a uniqueness the separates you from other people. Simply put, it is the "Who I am?" "What I am?" etc. When one struggles with choices and alternatives it can cause confusion. A variety of changes can affect one's work. See trying to overcome a problem or difficulty offers an opportunity to redefine who you are in terms of values, priorities and chosen lifestyle. Success in life is more than a goal; it is a journey, a day by day experience of achievement. Carpe diem, Latin for "seize the day" reminds us to live in the now because the present is the most valuable time we have.

In reinventing yourself you need to learn new skills in interpersonal relationships, the way you reach out to others and identify any of your behaviour patterns that need to be corrected. Through hard work and perhaps with some professional help it is possible to achieve some real changes. Progress is made in small steps.

Believe you can be different and much happier if you are truly willing to experiment and present a new image to your world. Remember if something is not working in your life you can do something about it. Through persistence and determination things can change.

Will the Real Me Please Stand Up

Personal identity is how you define yourself – who I am and what I am? Before you can start reinventing yourself and breaking out of your mould you need to ask yourself the following questions: -

Who am I? This is not an easy question. It does not refer to your role in life or what you do. It refers to the type of person you believe you are. Ask yourself: Am I happy and contented in life? Am I outgoing and enjoy interpersonal relationships? Am I warm and loving to those who are close to me? Do I express this love freely? Do I like the way I project myself and my personality? These and similar questions help you to identify who you are. Try a fresh approach and ask these questions.

What Roles Do I Play? In life you play many roles, let us explore some. If you are a parent or grandparent how do you feel about your role? In a work situation do you enjoy what you do? Do you feel comfortable with your roles as a caring and understanding human being? Do you take time to explore the spiritual aspect of your identity? Do you feel comfortable with your social, physical and cultural activities? Be proud of what you have already achieved and the role you play in life.

Where Am I Going In Life? Are you happy with the direction and activities your life offers you? Is your career direction clear to you? Are you marking time and going nowhere? Do you seem to be running around in circles? Are you proud of your success? What have you learned from life's failures? Are you in a dead end job with little opportunity for advancement? Remember these kinds of jobs may not lead anywhere but they do help to pay the bills. Take time to assess where you are heading in case you are being carried away by life's frenzy and paying too high a price. Look at ways to make life more enjoyable. Maybe you attract the wrong type of person into your life. Learn from these experiences.

Take time to reflect and ask yourself "What would I like to modify about my personality, attitude and emotional approach to life?" Once you have answered this question fix your response firmly in your mind and be prepared to work on changing those parts of yourself that do not work for you. Your life will be shaped by who you are and what you do. Be honest with yourself and live your life around your dream.

To achieve this you need to be fully aware of the reasons for making changes. It was Maxwell Maltz the author of "Psycho-Cybernetics" who developed a theory for reinventing oneself; he believed you can change anything in your personality if you are willing to work at it. Be prepared to give freely of yourself and show you care about others.

Dare to Be Different – Sort Out Priorities

Be brave in exploring what you want to change. Have realistic expectations and set goals toward achieving the desired result. Reinventing yourself is being willing to make those changes which will enhance your personality and improve your lifestyle. Become the person you were meant to be – release your hidden thoughts and feelings. Free yourself and be an experimenter.

While exploring new pathways any change you make needs to be consistent with your basic beliefs. Let your new image slowly emerge. Believe you deserve to be recognised for who you are. Remember, no one is perfect, but you are looking to change and be somebody who people accept and respect. Be convinced that you deserve the best life has to offer and do not accept second best.

You Become What You Focus On

In life what you focus on grows. Make sure you really know what you want from life. You think you know what will make you happy, for example, it could be more money, more possessions, the right person in your life, an employer who really appreciates your work and yet, even when this happens you still feel something is missing. There can still be an undercurrent of discontent. Some people are afraid of success and others have deep seated emotional problems that cause them to be unhappy.

Take time to go to a deeper level, that is, look past the superficial. You can do this through meditation, prayer, relaxation or listening to soothing peaceful music. Take time to relax. Write down the thoughts and concerns that emerge during this time of quiet reflection. Listen to your intuition and allow it to show you what needs to be addressed. Feel encouraged when you reflect on what could be. Be open to this period of reflection and introspection.

Creating a Visible Presence

You create a visible presence by what you say and do. Feel that you have something worthwhile to contribute to a conversation. Feel good about yourself. Let your body and words show you care. Respond to your gut feeling. Beam with confidence.

Instead of waiting for people to reach out to you, reach out to them and inquire about their world. Show genuine interest and concern for the wellbeing of others. Find some pleasure now even if the going is tough. Be proud, not arrogant about whom you have become because you have worked on yourself and feel that you now project a new visible presence. There is a new interest in the way you present yourself to others. How you think and feel shapes your life. Have aspirations that support your goals. Like what you are discovering and recognise inspirational and teachable moments.

Surprise Yourself – Do Something Out of Character

Surprise yourself and your friends by doing something you would not normally do. Jolt yourself out of your complacency. Be brave and accept the consequences of your action. Break predictable patterns. When this happens people will see you in a new light.

If you are a staid conservative person, experiment with life — change the way you dress, do a bungy jump, go on an unusual holiday, throw a theme party at your home, dress up in fancy costume and encourage others to follow your example. Your actions and attitude let people see you are different.

Many people would like to do something new or out of character but are afraid because they wonder what others will think. Enjoy the attention you receive. Use it to build your self confidence. You will notice people will change in their attitude to you and become closer. They will see you in a new light. Run some risks, without doing anything dangerous or unsafe, and notice the different way people respond.

Use Your Talents and Gifts

You will be encouraged to use your gifts and talents. Identify your strengths and accept your weaknesses. At times your talents get lost when problems of life seem to overwhelm you.

When you use these gifts and talents you feel that you are in control of your life. Never let anyone take these gifts away from you. At all times have a clear vision of your talents and gifts – make a list and keep it with you. Do something right now that helps you to become more actively aware of these special gifts and talents. Draw upon your unlimited imagination. Be prepared to express the real you. Handle your newfound freedom in a way that everyone benefits. This makes it easier for others to accept the new you.

Do Not Be Worried About What Others Think

The majority of people admire those who make a change in the direction of life providing it is a responsible decision. This is often referred to as a mid life crisis. It can come at anytime in your life. It was philosopher William James who said "The greatest discovery of my generation is that mankind can alter their lives by altering their attitude of mind". Explore and experiment and you will be surprised at what you can achieve.

If you believe there is still something else you want to do or a different way you want to live your life be prepared to have a go. If you never try you will always be disappointed about a lost opportunity. Often other people will not notice changes you are making as they are so lost in their own world. Some, however, look on with jealousy and wish they had the courage to make changes.

Experiment with your appearance and do not be afraid of what others think. Do what you believe is right for you. This applies equally to men and to women. This is a good place to start in reinventing yourself.

•

Not All Experiments Will Work

Recognise that not all the experiments you try will work, but some will be successful. Do not think you have failed but learn from the experience. At least you have been willing to try. Once you have embarked on this project the excitement and challenge will motivate you.

If you are finding a real obstacle be prepared to ask others for help. Tell these people what you are trying to do. Many are very willing to offer suggestions which could be helpful. You at all times must be accountable for the decisions you make. Study and listen to those around you. Keep up your momentum for change. Results are not always immediate.

Case Study

Tom's Story

Tom, a computer programmer with a large multinational company, had been married to Mary for three years. They had one child six months old.

He felt he was on top of the world until Mary told him she was unhappy and thinking about ending the marriage. Tom was sure it was post natal depression and nothing to do with him and suggested she see a doctor.

Two days later Mary wrote a letter explaining how she felt and what was wrong with the relationship. Tom found the letter in his briefcase. At first he was angry, hurt and felt it was unfair. After reading it four times he started to think differently. He asked his team leader for time off which was agreed upon.

That afternoon Tom and Mary had their most honest discussion ever. Mary was extremely lonely and love starved. She did not accuse Tom for all the mess the relationship was in and was prepared to accept 50% of the problem.

Mary said she talked with her doctor and it was suggested they both went to counselling. Tom did not want to share "his dirty linen" with someone else as he was a very private person. He also thought if he didn't relate to Mary how could he communicate with a perfect stranger? Mary insisted on counselling as she really wanted to save their marriage.

In the first interview Mary did most of the talking. Every once in awhile Tom might correct her or make a statement. I suggested that Tom might come to the next interview alone. He reluctantly agreed.

At the beginning of the interview Tom said "my mother always said never let your right hand know what the left hand is thinking". He said he had always lived by this rule. It worked well at work and he thought it was working at home.

I discussed with Tom a different approach to intimacy. I defined intimacy as "into-me-see". Tom was afraid of intimacy as people might use information supplied in confidence against him later. He was not one of those "touchy feelie" people. He kept his feelings to himself. I then started to explain that he and Mary lived in two different worlds. He did things but gave little of himself. He was a good provider and showed his love to his son who he could control but not to his wife. In his thinking he was sure that Mary loved him so why did he need to express it.

At the end of the interview Tom wanted to come back and explore what feelings and emotions were all about as this was a new discovery.

When Tom got home he fell into Mary's arms and said "I am an emotional failure". Mary was great with Tom and she shared her emotional needs and Tom listened. Next day he went to the library and picked up a book on feelings. He devoured it late into the night.

Tom in the last two months has made some major changes by sharing positive and negative feelings. He shares and expresses love freely even in front of others. He stands up at work for what he believes to be right. He is no longer a robot but a person in tune with himself and his feelings.

Personal Reflections

1. List five successes you have had over the past ten years. Remember it is what **you** call successful, however small the success may seem.

. . . .

. . . .

. . . .

. . . .

. . . .

2. If you could change anything about your identity, personality and self image, what would you change? Give details.

. . . .

. . . .

. . . .

. . . .

. . . .

3. Describe any feelings you have about reinventing yourself – positive or negative.

. . . .

. . . .

. . . .

. . . .

. . . .

. . . .

Action Strategies

Define yourself differently – be cheerful, happy, and slow to jump to conclusions.

Creativity, courage and change go together – see yourself succeeding in life by your willingness to make adjustments to your personality.

Be committed to improving your life – change requires effort and perseverance.

Act upon your convictions – do not let what others may think hold you back.

Your belief shapes your destiny – believe in your ability and give freely of yourself.

Give yourself permission to change.

Live wholeheartedly – be committed to being who you want to be.

Identify what does not work and change it.

Celebrate your achievements.

STRATEGY 4

How To Build Self Confidence and Self Esteem

Building Self Confidence

Self confidence and self esteem are extremely important in every aspect of our lives. Without them people find it difficult to succeed in life. Being self confident helps you to cope with the pressure of today's world. It does not happen naturally, but it can be learned and built on. It involves risk taking, choice and a willingness to experiment with yourself and life; being self-confident involves doing what you believe is right even if others criticize you, be willing to go the extra mile to achieve something, but it is also about balance between work and play and other activities. Be aware of being overconfident when you may take too many risks and stretch yourself beyond your capabilities and crash badly.

As you strive to improve, grow and achieve realistic goals, you start to feel better about yourself and this becomes more evident as your confidence grows. There is no guarantee that every decision you make will have a good outcome. Life has its ups and downs. Believe playing it safe and avoiding risks can be futile and produce much unhappiness and do very little in building self confidence. Focus on your achievements, no matter how small.

Anything worthwhile in life takes time and effort. New ideas take time to "seep" into your understanding before you can fully perceive them as your own. Often when you discover a new truth it may take some time before it becomes a reality. The new truth often has to fight the inner critic. New ideas, and new truths, keep you moving forward in life. Be open. Know that self limiting messages bring misery, unhappiness and destroy self confidence.

Adopt a Cheerful, Playful, Optimistic Approach

People are attracted to those with a cheerful disposition and who exhibit a high degree of self confidence. Adopt a happy, cheerful, playful and positive approach to life. Self confident people are positive people, and believe in themselves and their abilities. These people have found a way to cope with whatever happens by looking for the best in every situation.

You will notice these people have a smile on their face, a twinkle in their eye and always have a cheerful word of encouragement for others. They also have their bad days but they make the best of them.

It is great to be around such people as some of their enthusiasm and positive vibes rub off. They believe they have something worthwhile to share and offer it freely to others. They provide a welcoming and safe environment through the level of self confidence they express.

The Key To Healthy Self Esteem – Loving Yourself, Loving Others

The key to living confidently is being able to love yourself and love others. It is simply impossible to fully love others unless you first love yourself. Healthy self esteem based on this concept does not lead to arrogance or being egotistical. It is a way to respect yourself and others and to make your life worthwhile as you radiate joy and happiness.

You build your self esteem through self acceptance. Self acceptance allows you to recognise you are not perfect but accept yourself with all your strengths and weaknesses. Let go of the need to be right. Be your own best friend and become passionate about living.

Positive thinking and learned optimism combine to help you feel strong and confident about your life. Learned optimism helps you to face new learning experiences with confidence. Your self esteem helps you to look for the best in others. You come to know that you are as good as anyone else and others are as good as you. This helps to make each person in your life an equal. You have special gifts and talents and so have they. For you to advance you need to stick your neck out and trust your intuition. Feel a sense of inner satisfaction about what you are achieving.

Believe You Are Important

You are the most important person in your world but consideration at all times must be given to others. Once you accept this concept you will realise that you are the best person to help yourself. You need passion, purpose and resilience to bounce back from life's disappointments. You need to be excited about how you can change because you are accountable for your choices. Be proud of any achievements however small they may appear. Recognise you at least tried.

Create a positive internal environment whereby you believe you have something very worthwhile to give to family and friends. Believe that whatever happens, you will cope with the situation. Be excited about your change in attitude and the way you cope in building healthy self esteem.

Low Aim is Low Self esteem

If you have low self esteem you may have a low aim for your level of achievement. Your self limitations and negative self talk will hold you back because you want to fail or make a fool of yourself. Instead of thinking about how you failed, look at what you managed to do right in the situation. Prepare thoroughly for any task so that you can be sure you are ready. Work on any skills you need to improve your achievement level. You can never be over trained or too skilled for any challenge in life.

Set reachable goals for yourself and break difficult tasks into smaller steps. Reward yourself when you succeed, do not compare yourself with others no matter how small the achievement. Be yourself and accept that life is not a race against others. Run your own race and believe you can win. Keep repeating to yourself "Yes I can, and I will".

Do Not Sit Around and Wait For Things to Happen

For things to happen in your life you need to take full responsibility. There is no sense in sitting around and waiting for things to come your way. Value yourself as a person and do not let the past hold you back. Make a conscious effort to be different.

If you feel that you are shy and inferior to others around you know it is necessary to take some action to make some changes. It could be reading a book, attending a course, seeking professional help, talking to a friend or trying a new approach to life. Whatever it is you must be prepared to do something. It may be a trial and error approach but at least you are doing something. Life offers no guarantees but help often comes from unexpected sources. Your mission in life is to change those parts of yourself that hold you back.

Each new experience can teach you more about yourself. Life can at times seem mysterious and unpredictable but believe you can cope with life's tough blows. You may feel battered but you can bounce back and rise to the occasion with your self esteem intact. Be prepared to trust yourself and your judgments.

Be enthusiastic about what you are discovering about your self esteem and potential for living. Enthusiasm is the difference between winning and losing. Ralph Waldo Emerson reminds us that "Nothing great was ever achieved without enthusiasm". Look for a role model — someone who is enthusiastic, and learn from them. What is it they do that makes them enthusiastic, how do they act?

Limited Experiences Produces a Limited Life

When you play it safe and do not step out of your comfort zone you prepare yourself for a limited life. The way you grow is to show a willingness to try new things, to experiment with life and to discover some new things work. Free yourself from habits that limit progress.

Perhaps now is the time to extend your thinking and be willing to broaden your horizon and extend your range of activities. Some people are absolute perfectionists and are afraid of failure so activities are limited. Aim in life for improvement, not perfection. Create a new sense of individuality that lifts your spirit and builds self confidence. Feel that you really matter. Be prepared to move forward at your own pace as you become comfortable with your new identity.

Enjoy Who You Are and What You Do

If you are going to build self esteem and self confidence you need to enjoy who you are and what you do. Enjoy the changes you can see taking place in your life that are helping you to be more confident. Focus on what is uplifting and reach out to others. Believe you have something worthwhile to share. If you find this concept difficult use positive self talk to help you.

People will be attracted to you when they see you enjoying being yourself and what you do. Welcome new people who come into your life. Take time to cultivate new friendships and maintain old relationships.

Encourage others along the way. As you help others you will help yourself. Let love, peace and radiance flow from you to others. There will be times when you do not enjoy who you are and what you do but know that these times will pass and the positive feelings will come back. It was Flora Whittmore who said "The doors we open and close decide the lives we live".

Self Confidence Through Self Awareness

Inner security and belief in yourself helps you to keep your self esteem intact. Some people may be jealous of your achievements and the attention you receive. These people will do all they can to attack you for who you are and what you do. Value feedback. Assess it carefully. Listen to positive constructive thoughts that could help you at this time. Guard yourself against "put downs" when you know the criticism is untrue.

There is a tendency to attack people who are successful and seek to destroy their popularity. It is simply called "Knocking the Tall Poppy". Be both an interesting person and interested in others. Be proud of your progress.

Security is not found in things you do or your bank balance, it is a feeling you have about yourself. It is a feeling that is developed through thought and action. Start to challenge past negative experiences or messages by nurturing and caring for yourself in ways that show that you are valuable, competent, deserving and lovable. Care for yourself by getting enough sleep, eating nutritious food and exercising. Plan fun and relaxing things for yourself; reward yourself for your accomplishments and keep reminding yourself of your strengths and achievements. Forgive yourself when you fail to achieve all you hoped for.

Ten Practical Steps for Building Self Esteem

Remember That No One Is Perfect: Even the most confident people have insecurities. Acknowledge your insecurities and do something about them.

Be Assertive: Learn new skills that help you to assert yourself without being aggressive. Believe you have something worthwhile to contribute to life.

Show You Care: Practice common courtesies, kindness, encouragement and support when interacting with others.

Educate Yourself: As you look at your goals, identify the skills you will need to achieve them. Then look at how you can acquire these skills. Look for a program or course that fully equips you to achieve what you want to achieve, and ideally gives you a certificate that is accepted in your workplace.

Respect Yourself: The more you respect yourself, the more people will respect you. Be prepared to say "no" and not feel guilty. Recognise boundaries where you feel comfortable and do not allow yourself to be pushed. You decide when it is time to step out of your comfort zone – not someone else.

Do Not Undermine Your Self Worth: We are all different and each person is special in their own way. Admire admirable qualities in others; do not be jealous of them.

Live in the Present Moment: Do not let the past hold you back from enjoying the present. Change negative thoughts into positive ones. Make the best of each moment of each day.

Do Not Give Up on Your Dreams: To be without dreams is to live your life without a purpose. At first set small realistic dreams that are readily achievable. Think about your life so far, and list the five of the best things you've achieved. They could be that you came top in an important test or exam, played a key role in a team, produced the best sales figures in a period. Perhaps you did something that made a difference in someone else's life, did something to make someone smile or helped your family in some way. Think also about involvement in a community or cultural project or the way you help others.

Be Patient With Yourself: Do not be discouraged if at first you are not as successful as you hoped. Keep trying and believe eventually it will all come together. "Fake it" until you can "make it." Use positive self talk. Know there is more to life and you will never give up on yourself.

Personal Reflections

1. Describe the changes you feel that you are achieving in your life at the present time which help to build your self confidence and self esteem.

   . . . .

   . . . .

   . . . .

2. Take time to review your life in relation to self esteem in the following areas:

   Relationships: . . . .

   . . . .

   Work: . . . .

   . . . .

   Personality: . . . .

   . . . .

   Self Image: . . . .

   . . . .

   Other Thoughts: . . . .

   . . . .

3. Describe how you plan to improve your current level of self confidence.

   . . . .

   . . . .

   . . . .

   . . . .

Action Strategies

Learn to feel good about yourself and others.

Make an impressive impression – honour your individuality. Good self confidence and self esteem helps you to be noticed in today's world.

Shine from within – what you feel is more important than the way you look.

Know self confidence and self esteem are acquired skills.

Believe you can overcome shyness and inferiority and feel confident in today's world with hard work and belief in yourself.

Change your attitude and your mood – in life it is not what happens to you that is important but your attitude and response.

Treat yourself well – others will do the same.

STRATEGY 5

Believe In Your Uniqueness

There is No One Else Exactly Like You

You are unique. Know yourself well – your capabilities, resources and characteristics and your temperament.

You are a very special person and you need to believe it. Live your life fully but accept that it keeps changing. The choices you make along the way can prove to be refreshing and challenging. Explore and discover new ideas to enrich your life. Be open to meeting people who will present challenges and new thoughts to ponder. Reclaim your creative spirit. Gain personal satisfaction from what you accomplish.

Know your strengths and weaknesses. Feel that you have been placed in this world for a special purpose. Be proud of who you are and what you have already achieved. Let go of negative traits that hold you back from enjoying life. In order to become master of life it is necessary to become master of your thoughts. Be in tune with your own creativity and talents. Freely express the beauty of the inner self. Start creating your life from the inside out. Focus on things that really matter. Believe you can make a difference in the world.

People who believe in their own uniqueness look and feel important. They do not sell themselves short in describing their achievements. They associate with progressive people. As leaders they have a strong belief in themselves and are open and readily approachable.

Stepping Onto the Stage of Life

Believe life is for real and not a dress rehearsal. Many human beings never fully develop their talents or grasp opportunities because they fail to look at their world with new insights. These people just exist and never know the joy of fully living. They are locked up in their own insecure world.

No one is ever limited to one chance to enjoy life. Every day brings a new beginning but opportunities do not chase you, you have to look for them. In order to live life to the fullest, tap into your enthusiasm, excitement, intuition, insight, creativity, imagination and inspiration. All of these will lift your life to a new level. Get a new perspective on life and choose the way you wish to live. Create an exciting new lifestyle and study new evolving patterns which may take you in a new direction.

Unleash Your True Potential

Believe in your uniqueness as you build self confidence and personal identity. This helps you to discover your true potential. Finding your true self and true potential is the essence of life that changes existing into living. When you unleash your full potential you see life from a new perspective and face life's challenges with a sense of determination and inner confidence. Discover what is best for you and enjoy it. Like the discoveries you are making about life.

Believe thoughts are ideas which create your circumstances. Cultivate seed thoughts and ideas and see where they take you. No effort of yours is wasted. Each experiment has a message for you. Life is all about discovery, surprise and blazing your own trail. Remain open to the infinite possibilities the world has to offer. It is never too late to be who you want to be. Be addicted to living.

Success Is an Inside Job

Remembering that it is not what happens to you in life that really matters but your reaction towards what happens. Plan to do things better. Change your thinking pattern. Believe you can be happier than you are at the moment.

Success means overcoming negative thinking and this is an inside job, it is a matter of attitude. Success is the way you feel deep inside - a realization you can change.

Negative thinking is like a cancer eating away at your identity and leading to a fear driven life. Direct the energy of negative thought into a positive thought. If you find yourself visualizing failure, switch to success. If you hear yourself repeating negative words, change to positive ones. If you hear yourself saying, "I cannot", say to yourself, "I can". Accept one challenge at a time and do all you can to find the best solution. See each new experience as a positive learning experience which will help you on your way to better living. Once you are successful in solving a problem the next set of problems will not appear to be as hard.

Be Responsible for What You Say, Think and Do

Accept personal responsibility for all your thoughts and actions. Be proud of who you are and your own individuality. Trust tomorrow to be better than today as you grow with new understanding. Centre your life on thoughts that are uplifting and be prepared to speak out on issues that are important to you. Speak with confidence and conviction. People will be prepared to listen.

Listen to constructive criticism and analyse it to see if the points are valid. If they are, then be prepared to make changes.

Hold Onto Your Conviction – Strengthen Internal Resources

Be true to yourself: Believe in your convictions. Know what you feel and be prepared to stand up for your convictions. Cultivate inner wisdom by taking time to fully consider things that matter in your life. Be a thinking and doing person. Take time for inner reflections that help you to present a sensible viewpoint backed by logical argument. New goals give your life new meaning.

Recognise that not everyone will agree with your point of view. You know what is right for you. Be open and listen to what others have to say. Convictions are not set in stone but can change at any time as new information is presented. Be prepared to accept the consequences of your actions. Stand by your beliefs until you are given good reason to change.

Know who you are: Your convictions help you to come to a realisation of who you are. Value yourself as you reflect on the things that matter. Be prepared to share your convictions with those in the world around you, without being overbearing, pedantic or dogmatic. Simply encourage others to think about your opinions. Usually it is not what you say but how you say it that counts. Be gentle and touch the wisdom within.

Focus on Your Strengths and Use Them to Your Advantage

Become aware of your strengths so that at all times you can draw upon them and use them to your advantage. When life falls apart these strengths have a tendency to get lost and you need to be reminded that they are there for you to draw upon. Be prepared to eliminate destructive, disturbing thoughts and focus on positive strengths that rejuvenate and bring lasting peace and happiness. Be a person with a big heart and rise to the occasion. Visualise yourself succeeding.

Create a positive inner and outer environment in which you operate to help maintain your strengths and to feel, act and think with clarity of mind. You now have new insights that help you to act differently. Once you have created a strong habit of reacting in a positive way, it becomes a part of your personality and a character trait which enhances your life. Success is achieved in this area by doing small things well. These strengths then start to grow and affect major decisions in your life.

Your Purpose in Life is To Understand Yourself

In spite of all the trials and tribulations you pass through you are greater than you think. If you can accept this concept and apply it in your life you will see how it can work. Nature has given us the instinct to survive. Mankind has an inbuilt desire to be a survivor.

People express themselves through speech and feelings. Feel good about yourself in your heart and this will soon be evident to those around you. See each day as a new beginning. Be gentle with yourself.

You can live your life any way you choose. Through moments of inspiration and aliveness you will discover a way to become greater than you are. Each of us is in this world to express ourself fully and freely. The more you understand yourself, the better you understand others and accept them for who they are.

Negative thoughts and judgments limit full and free expression. Make it a habit to acknowledge and give thanks for everything. With this attitude of thankfulness you will be surprised to see how your life expands. Take time to reflect on this thought and value this special moment of insight. You know what is now important to you and look for the best in others.

Talk to yourself positively. Say to yourself, "I'm good", "I'm great", "I'm doing really well", "I am self confident"; feel good when you say these things to yourself.

Positive Reminders

1. **Have Confidence In Yourself And What You Are Doing.** Progress at times is made in small steps. Inch by inch life is a cinch. Your goals do not start in the brain but in the heart. Express your passion for living.
2. **You Can Make Life What You Want It To Be.** Life is for living and learning. You can learn life's lessons well and move on to the next. Celebrate your successes along the way. Treasure what you have discovered. Be proud of your achievements and never forget them.
3. **Believe You Are In A Period Of Transition.** It's not what you did that counts, or who you are at this stage, but who you are becoming. Change is growth and growth is life. Welcome this period of transition, tough as it may be, as one of the most significant periods of your life. Invent new ways of facing life's challenges. Be energetic and enthusiastic about your future as it evolves.

Case Study

Kimberley's Story

Kimberley had been in an unhealthy abusive relationship for five years. At work she was a force to be reckoned with as she held a responsible position as a financial controller. She was good at what she did and she knew it.

Kimberley was in her late twenties and could see her relationship was going nowhere. After a violent quarrel with her partner she walked out. When I saw her in counselling a week later she still had bruising and was very upset. Kimberley was an attractive woman but did not believe in her self and her beauty.

In personal relationships with men she became a little mouse. She did not want to rock the boat so she agreed to demands put upon her. She had only one close friend who brought her to counselling.

Kimberley soon recognised she was at a crossroad - either go back into the abusive relationship or make a fresh start. She said “the devil you know is better than the one you don’t know”. I asked her if this is the way she solved business problems and she instantly stood up and said “I certainly do not”.

At the end of the interview Kimberley decided to think about what she wanted from the relationship. She decided to ask her partner Keith to go counselling. Keith became violent again and ordered her out of the apartment and said “He never wanted to see her again”.

Kimberley worked on her personal identity. She was quick to point out that her mother had instilled into her that to look into a mirror was vain. Her mother disliked the way she dressed and told her she looked cheap and common. Keith never gave her any compliments or noticed how she dressed.

Her relationship with men changed. Kimberley knew that she had a lot to offer in a relationship and also knew what she wanted. She was enthusiastic about life and was reaching out freely to others. There was a real change of attitude and she was now a person in her own right and excited about her future.

Personal Reflections

1. Describe five talents you believe you have. How are they used in your life to express your uniqueness?

   . . . .

   . . . .

   . . . .

   . . . .

   . . . .

2. To improve your lifestyle list five skills you would like to acquire and why?

   . . . .

   . . . .

   . . . .

   . . . .

   . . . .

3. List five strengths and five weaknesses which you would like to address.

   Strengths:. . . . .

   . . . .

   . . . .

   Weaknesses: . . . .

   . . . .

   . . . .

   . . . .

Action Strategies

Value each moment. Act on it, live it—grab magical moments of inspiration.

Do what you like to do – set a new course, shift your focus, and set new goals.

Too much comfort makes life too boring – let go of ways that no longer serve you.

Appreciate your uniqueness of individuality – you are a person in your own right. Believe that you are special.

Each day offers new challenges, new opportunities – be prepared to face these challenges and do your best to overcome them.

Know what you can become and achieve—expand your circle of influence.

Catching up on living – give yourself something to look forward to. Life is an incredible gift.

STRATEGY 6

Positive Optimism – Believe The Best Is Yet To Be

Positive Optimism Ignites your Passion for Living

Optimism is about attitude and ignites a belief that helps you view the world as a positive place. It helps you to discover an approach to life that is creative, productive and enjoyable. You become passionate about what you want from life. You realise that you too can become successful.

This approach creates a hopeful state of mind and is valuable in difficult situations. Instead of running away from a challenge or confrontation you have the opportunity to learn some new skills. Let your life unfold in a new way through positive optimism, perseverance and determination.

Optimism takes you out of a world of insecurity and encourages independence and an outgoing attitude, which in turn fends off depression and anxiety. It helps you change negative ingrained thinking patterns and transform them into positive beliefs. A new learning pattern develops which stops you filling your mind with negative thoughts.

With this approach to life you get things done by directing time, effort, energy and believing in constructive and positive thinking. Remember the more you put into life the more you get out of life. Do what you can today to solve a problem. See problems as possibilities for growth.

Eliminate Negative Thinking

Being optimistic is a choice that you and only you can make; your feeling good does not depend on external circumstances, but on what you choose to think.

Instead of approaching a problem with a closed mind, be flexible and open to new thoughts and ideas that help you to find a positive solution. Tackle one problem at a time. Explore alternatives and break up a problem into small manageable sections. Be committed to a positive outcome. Know what you have to do to improve your decision making skills.

As you become mentally flexible see the possibilities for good in all of life's situations. You have only one life so make the best of it. Invest in yourself, in education, development of ideas, and put 100% into what you do. Results in life come in proportion to enthusiasm and time invested in a project.

This positive approach offers hope in life's most difficult situations. Growth takes place when you focus on a positive outcome. Face events with a positive frame of mind to make life easier and more enjoyable.

Unhappiness can be overcome by having a positive attitude to life. It takes time and effort. Clearly identify what you want to change and be prepared through reading, sharing and reflecting to make the necessary changes. Improve your life by improving your thinking.

Remove Yourself From Negative Influences

Your environment begins to reflect who you are after time. If you have friends or people at work you regularly associate with who are always whingeing about their job, boss, or life then begin to slowly weed out that group of people and seek out those who are positive, and don't talk about others behind their back. Replacing a negative environment with a positive one, you begin to improve your own life.

How To Get Ahead In Life

Be prepared to explore new pathways that could enrich your life. Believe every new set of circumstances offers a unique opportunity for growth. Practise enjoying life. See the way around an obstacle. Tough times teach us valuable lessons.

Periodically during the day, stop and evaluate what you're thinking. If you find that your thoughts are mainly negative, try to find a way to put a positive spin on them. When your state of mind is generally optimistic, you're able to handle everyday stress in a constructive way.

You are equipped to deal with challenges and to find solutions. Think and act like a winner.

Inside every one of us is a very wise person. This is the silent observer, the knowing internal guide that is available to each of us. Psychologists, poets, philosophers use different words to describe this inner guide but all agree that the inner guide exists. Communicate with this inner wisdom by being still, meditating and listening.

Lifetime Learning Keeps You Motivated

From the cradle to the grave life is for living and learning. Positive optimism is a way of replacing outdated negative attitudes that hold you back from enjoying life. No one needs to stay stuck. With your new found hope, belief in yourself and new skills, believe you can find a solution.

Be prepared to admit some of the beliefs and attitudes you have picked up through life may not have been productive. Recognise that you can choose to move from negative thinking to positive thinking and open up to a new world.

No longer look at a very difficult situation and see it as impossible. Free up your mind to see possible solutions. Feel different in your life and realise that you are no longer bogged down but are experiencing a new found freedom.

Remember every big accomplishment is a series of little ones along the way. Optimistic people put heart and soul into what they do. Without dreams and goals people lack a clear direction in life. Use positiveness to turn setbacks into victories. Defeat is only a state of mind.

Ask for what you want in life and do all you can to achieve it. You may not always get what you ask for but you are in a better position to cope with what comes your way

Creating Your World of Reality

You create your own world of reality as you believe what you do really matters. Each person has the opportunity to become successful through their skill, energy and ability providing they are prepared to make adjustments where necessary. Recognise that there may be more to life than what you are getting.

Optimism grows with persistence and experimentation. If one approach does not work then find another way. What is needed is the accumulation of ability and ambition to seek a solution. Most good ideas develop from making adjustments along the way.

People may be divided into three groups: (1) those that make things happen (2) those who watch things happen, and (3) those who wonder what is happening. To create a world that makes you happy be one of those people who make things happen. It is only by taking action that you learn what works and what does not work. Have courage and be willing to try, and notice the difference.

Believe you have the ability to create your world. In a way there is a similarity to the game of cricket. You cannot play well unless you first know how to bat, bowl and field. In life you cannot create your world unless you know what the game is all about, or the rules. It is not the lack of skills which keeps most people off the playing field of life; it is something inside them. Perhaps fear of failure prevents positive action. People can be their own worst enemy. Believe in yourself. The time to begin is now. Acknowledge any fears but be a person of action. Life is too short to wait.

Develop a New Approach to Life

If you are unhappy with your approach to life, here is an opportunity. Look to make some changes. Ask yourself "is there a better approach to obtain a better result?" Come to terms now with what you are capable of achieving. Be optimistic about your life. Be prepared to stretch yourself and learn new skills.

Life comes without instructions. There are no guarantees. There are hazards and risks along the way. Try as hard as you might, you will be unable to eliminate all risks from life. Do not let doubt or fear hold you back from trying a different approach to life. You have much to gain from the experience and can see fresh opportunities as you move forward. Be prepared to be surprised.

Life offers hope and encouragement as you believe in yourself and others. Positive people know what they want from life and what they have to give to life. Goals give them energy and enthusiasm to pursue their dreams. Such people act on an idea and are not afraid of failure.

Simply make up your mind to change your thinking. Instead of "It won't work", say "I will give it a try". Instead of "It's too complicated" say "I'll try it from a different angle". Remember, "Yes I can, and I will".

Become A Student Of Human Nature

Life Is For Learning: Learn from every experience. Watch how others operate and learn from them. No one knows you better than yourself. Decide what is best for you. The possibilities for learning are unlimited.

Focus On What Is Important: Recognise what is important in your life and build it into all your activities. Engage with life and be prepared to explore opportunities that come your way. Never run away from a challenge. Make use of newly acquired knowledge and put this into practice. If you use the knowledge you will never lose it.

Kindness To Self And Others: Show kindness, encouragement and support to others. At the same time learn how to be kind to yourself and never be afraid to say no to others. Be prepared to accept the consequences of your actions.

Grow Through Loss: Loss is experienced in many ways. It could be the loss of a partner through divorce or death, the loss of a child, the loss of a job, loss through drug addiction or poor communication skills. Then there is also financial loss, the loss of self esteem, the loss of direction and many more losses. In each case a loss can be a time of growth depending on how you respond to the challenge. Be resilient, make adjustments and bounce back.

Breaking Fear Patterns: Recognise fear patterns that cause you worry and anxiety. Replace fear with faith and belief in yourself. Let go of old habits and learn to face problems with a positive attitude. Discard old rules that no longer suit your way of life. Any setback provides a valuable learning experience. Life's choices, changes, and challenges are there to bring out the best in you.

Personal Reflections

1. On the scale below, rate your level of positive optimism and have you reached this decision

   1 2 3 4 5 6 7 8 9 10

   . . . .

   . . . .

2. Describe any fear or negative thoughts that hold you back from achieving a positive outlook on life

   . . . .

   . . . .

   . . . .

   . . . .

   . . . .

   . . . .

3. Name three things you can do immediately to change your negative thinking which will help you to achieve your goals

   . . . .

   . . . .

   . . . .

   . . . .

   . . . .

   . . . .

   . . . .

   . . . .

Action Strategies

Find new pathways – live with energy and be willing to explore and experience a different approach to life's challenges.

Expand your thinking...pathways...capacity for living – positive optimism helps you to reach out and expect the best life offers and help you acquire new skills.

Overcome boredom – stop vegetating. Identify what is missing and do something about it.

Improve your quality of life – lift your life to a new level with new possibilities.

Look for new strategies to improve your outlook on life – look for new strategies - be willing to explore new pathways. Some paths will come to a dead end but keep exploring.

Revive and come alive— believe there is more to living and be excited about the possibility of positive outcomes.

Develop a daily success ritual – be thankful for what you have. Count your blessings. Show gratitude to others. Be thankful for people who wish to help you.

STRATEGY 7

Stop Procrastinating – Make Good Decisions

To Be Or Not To Be

Decisions are at the heart of success, but they can be difficult, perplexing, and nerve racking. The difficult part is to pick one solution where the positive outcome outweighs possible losses. Avoiding decisions often seems easier. Yet making your own decisions and accepting the consequence is the only way to stay in control of your success, and your life.

We all know the difference between “right” and “wrong”, and we can tell “good” from "bad". But we also know that the more difficult decisions come when we have to choose the better of two options. Decision making is a courageous act that entails opting for various courses of actions that will determine one’s success.

Factors that contribute to good decision making include self esteem, confidence and the courage to do what you are afraid of doing. Be honest about who you are and what you wish to achieve, and how you care about yourself and others who might be affected by your decisions.

Overcome Procrastination with the Right Attitude

Some people find it extremely difficult to make decisions. The dictionary defines procrastination as "delaying action". This is putting off things until another time, or the right time which may never come. When one is afraid of making decisions or does not know how to decide, there is a tendency to procrastinate. This then becomes a habit.

To change from procrastinator to an action oriented problem solver is to believe in your ability to face life's challenges. Believe that most decisions you make will work well. Mistakes should become learning experiences and help you to grow as an individual. Once you start to make decisions in small matters it becomes easier with bigger decisions. It is true, getting started is the hardest. But once you start, momentum will pick up and before you know it, the task is done! Determine a time for making a decision and the criteria for making it. Share your deadline with someone else.

Procrastination can be overcome with the right attitude. Recognise that it is a habit that can be changed with persistence, belief in self and a change in mindset. You need to admit you are a procrastinator and to be ready to do something about it. No one can make the decision for you.

Start by seeking to accomplish small tasks before you attempt the big ones. Get yourself better organised for the task at hand. Some people find great difficulty in organising themselves and wait until they are in the mood. When you complete a task give yourself a reward. Do not be afraid to ask for help. Even if you are having a hard time in completing a project take a break and promise yourself you will complete it sometime later – before the end of the day if possible.

Do Not Suffer In Silence

There is no need to suffer in silence because you do not know what to do with a problem. Be prepared to ask for help. Encourage your friends to be truthful in their remarks. They may see things from a new perspective, different from your point of view, offering a new insight. Identify the problem to be solved. Generate ideas for possible solutions by brainstorming with others.

If you are lonely or suffering from some illness, find a support group. Be prepared to attend the group for at least three or four sessions before you decide to stay or leave. Feel that you have something worthwhile to contribute and to receive from the group. Practice simple acts of kindness even if they go unnoticed. Show your gratitude for any help you might receive. Take the initiative and use new found skills and encourage others.

The Essence of Good Decision Making

Collect all the information, for and against, when making a decision. Never make a decision when you feel agitated or out of control. Consider the effect of your decision upon others.

When you know what you really want from life it becomes easier to make decisions. You can develop a plan of action which will help you achieve your goals. Approach a problem with an open mind. Be prepared to be inconvenienced and uncomfortable as you search for answers. Be creative and imaginative as you think through the problem and find some possible solutions. Test these out and see where they will take you. Life at times can be trial and error.

Define a problem and write it down in no more than 50 words. Next decide on any immediate action you can take. Evaluate each choice in terms of its consequences. Use your values and judgment criteria to determine the pros and cons. Attempt to evaluate the possible outcome of your decision. What lessons can be learnt?

This is an important step for further development of your decision making skills and judgment. Decide whether the risk is necessary or desirable. Spend time in some careful thought before acting, so that you will not end up taking unnecessary risks. If you are feeling angry, hurt, depressed, desperate, revengeful or frightened resist making a decision.

Set up a timetable with a list of steps to take. Use the plan as a guideline, but be flexible. When you have evaluated the risk and decided that it's worth it, act decisively. Once you get going, be courageous. Grit your teeth and move forward. Do not procrastinate but make sure you have all the information available which could shed new light on the situation to bring about a change of direction.

Do Not Develop an Ostrich Complex

The "Ostrich Complex" is burying your head in the sand and hoping that the problem will go away. If you ignore a problem it will soon fester and become more complex. People with this ostrich complex trick themselves into denying that the problem exists and therefore believe there is nothing to be concerned about. These people go merrily on their way until eventually the problem catches up with them and they feel overwhelmed by the situation.

Feel the Fear

It is normal to feel fearful when called upon to make a major decision. You know that a decision has to be made. If another person is involved you need to take time to listen to their views and to give them time to do any research that may be needed. If there is too much time there will be a sense of "stewing" over the problem which can lead to confusion. Decide on the length of time needed to make the best decision.

Use Creative Thinking for Problem Solving

Progress in problem solving is made in small steps. It was Robert Schuller who said "Inch by inch life is a cinch", and this applies to problem solving. No one else is going to solve your problem but yourself. There is no magical formula to make problems disappear.

Use Positive Affirmations: Write down on a piece of paper the affirmation "I am now open to positive solutions (... state the problem as succinctly as possible ...)". Writing down the affirmation helps to actualise the solution. Using creative visualisation or developing a clear mental picture of the completed task, or how you want to be in life will help you maintain a focus on the end result, not just the process. Remind yourself how good you'll feel when you're finished. .

Decisions Define Your Future

The decisions you make can affect your future. The way you think about yourself affects the way you act and react. Your decisions about your goals and beliefs affect the way you view life and all it has to offer. It is your attitude which will strengthen or weaken your decision-making process.

Life is not accountable to you, realise you are responsible for the way you use your life. You need to recognise your unique possibilities. Make your own decisions about who you are and what you hope to become rather than allowing others decide for you. Explore and expand the power of your mind. The great thing about life is not where you are but where you are heading.

It is far better to attempt a worthwhile project than to stand on the sidelines of life with a wait and see attitude. Only you can open the door to your future or shut it because of fear. In other words you choose your world and what it will be like.

Structures & Strategies For Problem Solving

Focus On What Is Working: Recognise what is working in your life and work from your strengths. Instead of complaining about what you do not have, appreciate what you do have. Recognise your gifts and talents and use them to move forward in your life.

Revive Sagging Spirits: When the pressures of life build you may feel dejected and become fearful and depleted in energy. The way you revive your sagging spirits is to increase your energy level. Be involved in a physical exercise program, such as walking, swimming, or some other sporting activity or be involved with a group of caring positive people. Find something you can do for someone else, for example, a visit, a phone call or some act of kindness. You will benefit from these activities. Take time to see the natural beauty around you and become involved with nature. Go for a walk and appreciate the beauty you discover along the way.

If your spirits are still sagging talk to a friend honestly about the way you feel. If nothing changes, be prepared to seek professional help.

Take Charge Of Your Life: Instead of being indecisive, be prepared to take personal responsibility for all your actions. Seek your true purpose in life no one else can give it to you. Listen to what others say but you make your own decisions. Learn to trust yourself and your decisions. Search for meaning and recognise what you have to do. Learn that there is a softer way to make a hard hitting comment. Life is a precious gift and each of us needs to value this gift. Be prepared to slow down your pace of life in order to catch up with yourself. At times it may appear that you are going so fast that you end up going around in circles. Procrastination and fear are the two strongest factors that hinder decision making. Change your thinking; make positive statements about your life. Be action oriented.

Case Study

Anne's Story

Anne was one of those people who had difficulty in making a decision, whether to buy a dress, what to cook for dinner, or even when to phone a friend. Anne had lost her way in life and felt she was almost invisible.

Anne eventually decided to seek help through counselling. Anne said she was a born procrastinator "I felt hopeless, desperate and even thought of suicide, I had no real option, I knew I needed help".

I explained to Anne that she still had freedom of choice in such a difficult situation. I was also quick to point out that some desperate people never seek help and that she was to be commended.

Anne had a Bachelor of Science. She had been married for 18 years and had three children 16, 14, 12. Her husband had a prosperous accountancy practice. He was an extremely quiet man but very dominant and actively engaged in the children's sport and he was away four nights a week and some weekends at seminars or other business functions. There was very little conversation.

Some months previously Anne employed a private investigator to trace her husband's movements. She was suspicious as she overheard one of her husband's "mysterious" phone calls. Her fears were confirmed within a couple of days when she was given a detailed report of her husband's movements. From that time on she became very insecure and expected her husband to leave the marital home any day. Their sex life ended four years previously and was never discussed. Anne said "I am a complete wreck" but insisted she still loved her husband.

I suggested that perhaps her husband wanted the best of both worlds — his home and an affair on the side.

I asked what Anne wanted from life and without hesitation she said “I would love to do research in a medical laboratory”. Her face changed, the voice strengthened with conviction. She discussed the issue with her husband who thought the idea was ridiculous but in spite of his opinion she eventually found a position. Although it was not exactly what she wanted but saw it as the beginning of a new life.

It was a beginning in more ways than one. Anne had to buy new clothes for her working life. She had to report once a week about her research. A week’s menu had to be prepared in advance and family members given additional tasks. She and her husband began communicating about their relationship and within about six weeks they discussed their sex life.

The husband stopped going out at night and the relationship started to flourish. Anne enrolled in a course which will help to improve her research. She fits well into the team at work and has become very decisive. She never told her husband about the information she gained from the private investigator. Anne faced a challenge and made some wise decisions to bring about change in her life and her relationship by working on her-self.

Anne is now a different person and is decisive and assertive. Her attitude to life has changed radically and her husband wants to rebuild the relationship. Anne at this time is deciding whether she will stay in the marriage or move out.

Personal Reflections

1. Describe in 100 words the approach you take to decision making.

. . . .

. . . .

. . . .

. . . .

. . . .

. . . .

2. If you are a procrastinator state what you can do to change this situation.

. . . .

. . . .

. . . .

. . . .

. . . .

. . . .

3. If you can identify with the 'ostrich concept', decide what are you going to do to change?

. . . .

. . . .

. . . .

. . . .

. . . .

Action Strategies

Learn to think creatively in decision making - look for the best outcome. Think outside the square. Explore new ways of thinking.

Decisions affect destiny - see the long term outcome.

Be prepared to be action oriented - overcome the avoidance factor.

Tap into the wisdom within—seek solutions. All the answers to life are within us.

Ask for help—listen to others - make your own decisions.

See all sides of the problem - to make a good decision be prepared to see both sides, positive and negative.

Turn a challenge into an opportunity for growth.

STRATEGY 8

Waking Up To Life – Life is For Living

Believe There Must Be More to Living

An inner restlessness indicates that you are still searching for something that will make your life complete. It is good to be able to stop and question what you are getting from life and acknowledge that something could be missing and that you need to modify your life or your attitude to life in some way. What do you really want out of life? Think long and hard, because this is *your* future.

Searching For What is Missing

Some people drift lazily through life without a sense of purpose. Others keep themselves busy every waking moment but life still feels empty. Then there are others who do nothing but compare themselves unfavourably with friends and neighbours. However, there are a group of successful people who have discovered something very important, that it is up to the individual to make things happen in their lives. These people ask an important basic question "There must be more to life than I am getting?" This question opens the door to honest thinking, experimentation and exploration of new areas of activity.

Existing Or Living

Life is what you make it. The main difference between existing and living is that in existing you let life control you, with living you are in control of your life. Some people merely exist in a rut that may even seem comfortable. This existence becomes a matter of habit and one day runs into the next with monotonous regularity. For those who are passing through a crisis this behaviour is all about survival and is acceptable until they are ready to move on to the next stage of living.

Exciting changes happen when you are open to new ideas that help you to explore the world around you. You need to develop a zest for living; a sense of passion and an inexhaustible enthusiasm to enjoy the best life has to offer. Develop the art of curiosity and be willing to explore the world around you.

Live Your Life In The Present Moment

New Moments: The only moment you really have is the present moment and you need to make the most of it. Having said that, you do need to think and plan for the future. Each moment is a new one.

The present moment may be cheerless and hurting. You need to feel and express the pain and know in time it will pass away. Life is made up of pain and pleasure. It is often very complex. Emotional hurt can often be manifest as physical pain. Pain in your body is an indication that something is wrong and you need to talk to your doctor.

Are You Fun To Be With? Are you a happy person and reflect this by the way you live? Happy people complain less. They have a lot of nice things to say about others. Fun people have their trials and disappointments but learn to accept them and bounce back.

These people get as much pleasure out of life as possible. They know what works for them in relationships and use these positive qualities. Much enjoyment is expressed in meeting new people and enjoying their company and keeping old friends.

Appreciate The Sounds Of Silence: In the journey of life you need moments of stillness when you can recharge your batteries. You can be lost in your own thoughts or a world of make believe.

Living in the present moment does not mean that you have to be active every minute of every day. It is being in tune with what your body needs at this precise moment. You can run your life ragged by continuous activity and push your body so hard. Stop before you are forced to.

Find a place in your home, at the beach or in the country where you can be alone with your thoughts and to be in tune with God and nature. Visit this spot on a regular basis.

Small Moments Are Important: Take time to appreciate the beauty around you such as the smile or words of a small child. Recognise the little courtesies that are extended to you, a gentle touch, a smile, a kind word or some small meaningful gesture that touches you deeply. Once you recognise them, accept and feel these moments, they will linger in your memory.

Recognise Precious Encounters: Do not dismiss brief, unexpected events; these could have an important impact upon you. It is often these moments that have a far greater impression upon you than major achievements. Become more aware of people who cross your path for even a fleeting moment. They may say a word or two to make you stop and think. These precious moments can be of great value, see them as teachable moments.

Giving and Receiving

Some people are excellent at giving but very poor at receiving because of a lack of self esteem. These people feel embarrassed and unworthy to receive recognition.

In a relationship some people give, in order to control. This type of person uses any means to dominate a relationship. Some give expensive gifts to build a relationship as they believe by doing so people will then like them, but they find it difficult to give of themselves. Often the weakest link in a relationship controls whatever happens.

It is great to be generous towards yourself and others. If you give freely the universe has a way of repaying you for your kindness in a most unexpected way. People love a cheerful giver – a person who gives for the right reasons.

Put Yourself Into What You Do

To make a real connection with others you need to believe in yourself and what you do and what you say. Words need to be backed up by actions. People need to feel your presence through your words and genuine concern. Give the best you have to life and you will find life gives you back far more than you put into it. Life is a school and a teacher. Try to be the best you can at what you do. Be open and flexible.

Be Open to New Ideas

Some people approach life with a closed mind. Be positive and approach life with an open mind and be inquisitive and interested in new ways of doing things and the possibilities that surround you. It is all in the matter of attitude.

You know by now that life is created in the mind by the way you think. You will experience what you create in your mind. It will be evident in your life. To reach your full potential you need to keep exploring…keep discovering…keep striving and keep growing.

Believe you have, right now, the opportunity to become successful in your own right by using your skills, energy and natural ability.

You change things around you when you start changing yourself and your attitude to life. “As a man thinketh so he is” - this old proverb is so true today. You are responsible for the construction of your life, so be open to new ideas that help you on the pathway to success.

Fixing Up Your Life Is An Inside Job

In life it is not what happens to you that counts, but the way you respond. This response comes from inside. Your emotional response comes from the way you feel about yourself deep down in your soul or that part which you refer to as your spirit. As you wake up to life you see new ways to enrich your life which adds a new dimension and this could be by finding and exploring the spiritual component of your life.

Fixing your problem from the outside is like putting a band aid on a sore without treating the cause. Changing your job, your partner, your car and your friends may help for awhile but it is only temporary. Real change comes through emotional and psychological understanding based on the ability to understand and find solutions for your problems. You need to stop and analyse who you are and how you could respond better to life’s challenges. It is all about extending your horizons and seeing life’s opportunities for fun, enjoyment, and real living.

Discover What Life Is All About

Right Thinking: Right thinking must stand up to logical questioning. It is based upon the best information available. The more effort you put into life with right thinking, the more you are likely to get out of life. Effort coupled with a winner's attitude is a great prescription for happiness. Right thinking is telling yourself and believing the words "I am ready and willing to discover what life is all about". Right thinking drives out the loser mentality which says "poor me, nothing good ever happens to me". It is waking up and breaking out of your cocoon.

Negativity saps your energy and fear takes over. Positive thinking allows you to see progress. Appreciate your achievements however small they may be.

Well Done Is Better Than Well Said: In life you need less talk and more action. Words need to be backed up by actions. It is so easy to talk the talk. Society appreciates people who are prepared "to have a go". There are no mistakes in life, only learning experiences if you are prepared to stop and take responsibility for your actions and reactions. You can learn from every situation. Aim for action not excuses. Believe a challenge will bring out the best in you and you will find a way to rise to the challenge and not be defeated by the excuses you put forward.

You Are A Product Of Your Thoughts: What you focus on grows in your life. If you let fear and negativity rule your life you will view it from a negative viewpoint and expect the worst. What you look for you usually find. Positive thoughts generate positive energy and you begin to see life differently. Start using this approach to life by looking for the best in yourself and others. Build on your gifts and talents so that they become stronger and help you move forward.

Exude Confidence: Exude confidence by the way you dress, speak and relate to others. Send positive vibrations to others. Be joyful, happy, and share this with others. Recognise that losers, on the other hand, can drain even positive people by their strong negative reactions. Choose to be with positive people.

Believe The Best Is Yet To Be

Feel excited about the possibilities that are ahead of you. Acknowledge that your approach to life has not worked and that you are now ready to try something new. You are not prepared to let life slip by and be a spectator, you are ready to be a participator in the game of life. Believe you have the strength, the knowledge and the get up and go to make things happen. Realise that you have been existing and not living. Know there is a lot of catching up for you to do.

Personal Reflections

1. Write about three activities you believe could enrich your life.

. . . .

. . . .

. . . .

. . . .

. . . .

. . . .

2. Describe any lessons you are learning from the "University of Hard Knocks".

. . . .

. . . .

. . . .

. . . .

. . . .

. . . .

3. Describe how you feel as you wake up to a new world of new learning experiences.

. . . .

. . . .

. . . .

. . . .

. . . .

Action Strategies

Assess your priorities—priorities keep changing. Determine what is important to you at this time of life.

Wake up to life — it is being involved, engaged and making your own decisions.

Be internally motivated – usually what you think you create in your life.

Discover your passion – see life as a voyage of discovery. Be passionate about the changes you want to make.

Experience the joy of aliveness – grab hold of your dreams. Be happy, be joyful. You are no longer a spectator as you awake to a new world.

Life is not a dress rehearsal – stop existing and start living.

STRATEGY 9

Success and Personal Motivation – Setting Realistic Goals

Recognise Opportunities

To become self motivated you need to think outside the square. Being creative involves using your imagination and risk taking skills. The self motivator believes in his ability for adventure and leadership and is open to new ideas and willing to experiment. The movers and shakers of the world respond positively to a challenge. They look for opportunity and realise that it does not come knocking at their door.

Go the Extra Mile

People who want to translate their dreams into action are willing to go the extra mile and work smarter, not longer. These people embrace all life has to offer and recognise those inspirational moments when a seed of an idea begins to germinate. When these special moments occur, quickly write them down otherwise they could be lost.

Success and Enthusiasm

The key to successful motivation is enthusiasm. Enthusiasm is an incredibly powerful tool to create momentum. It can also be used to combat fear and nervousness. Being enthusiastic also creates an overall feeling of happiness and well-being that makes it worthwhile regardless of its positive side-effects. In the game of life enthusiasm can mean the difference between winning and losing. Ralph Waldo Emmerson said "Nothing great was ever achieved without enthusiasm". It is the one small ingredient that can make such a difference as you face life's challenges.

Enthusiasm is like any other skill. If it is continually practiced and exercised, it gets better. An enthusiastic person is able to overcome obstacles that come their way. These people believe in themselves and the projects that they are involved in. This enthusiasm helps them to move along and not become bogged down by difficulties.

Mix with Motivated People

Motivated people are those who have their feet on the ground and have a positive approach to everyday life. They are willing to try a variety of options to get what they want rather than keep hitting their head against the same brick wall. They are willing to take risks, are energetic, they possess an attitude of success and are persistent. They are willing to share their success secrets with others.

Find yourself lacking in some of these areas? Identify others you know who possess these traits and ask them to guide you or find out how they went about developing these attributes. Make a concerted effort to integrate the traits of highly motivated people into your behaviours, and you'll be amazed at how much more you can achieve in your personal and professional life

Read stories about successful men and women. Attend motivational seminars and make an investment in your potential for living. The average person uses between 5 - 10% of their potential. There is so much more within you waiting to be released.

Give Yourself Permission to Succeed

Some people are afraid of success because they know success brings with it responsibilities. Success requires effort and willingness to run some calculated risks. Then there are a group of people who believe they are born losers and have a loser mentality. These people are fear controlled and do not wish to change. Once you give yourself permission to succeed your life changes. It does not mean you will be an overnight success but if you are prepared to alter the way of doing things and are willing to learn new rules about life things can change to your advantage.

To succeed you need inspiration and a plan of action. You can be inspired by what others have achieved. You may feel a compelling urge to lift your life to a new level. Once you are inspired you need a plan of action to take you to your next step. Make sure your plan is achievable and measurable. Once there is inspiration and action you will become motivated and life will gradually change as you reach for new dreams.

Simple Rules for Successful Achievement

Results Are Not Always Immediate: Although you might like what you do and are gifted, the results are not always immediate. Blend together drive, determination and persistence to succeed.

Develop a "Do It Now" Attitude: Put procrastination behind you. You cannot live your life backwards. A person with an "I can do it attitude" is the one who gets results.

Believe You Are Above Average: You have a healthy self esteem and are unique in your own right; you are a somebody. Believe you can be an exceptional person in times of accomplishment as well as in adversity. Find the niche that helps you to build a better world for yourself and others.

Stand by Your Integrity: Do not lower your standards but hold true to your basic beliefs. People admire those who live by their convictions. Stand tall and be proud of your accomplishments.

Dare to be Different: People who are successful stand out from the crowd. They are not conservative but adventurous and are trail blazers. They have learned about the abundance that the universe offers.

Expect a Miracle in Unexpected Situations: Miracles still happen today. Be smart enough to recognise them. Miracles happen at the right time. Through the synchronicity of life, rewards can come from the most unexpected sources. This is not a coincidence but a reward from the concept "what you sow you reap".

Know What You Want and Go For It: Some people have a strong desire to accomplish and are prepared to make sacrifices along the way to achieve their dreams. They seek new insights to help them reach their true potential.

Successful Business Principles: If in business, be smart enough to employ people with strengths that complement yours. You then can concentrate on activities which allow you to use your strengths. Actively affirm the unique qualities you see in yourself and others. Be generous with compliments.

Your Most Important Asset: You can be the most successful person in the world but without your health and friends, your success can be empty. Take time to care for your body, make sure that you eat the right food and have proper exercise. Everything in moderation helps the body to function optimally. Appreciate meaningful friendships and show your gratitude.

Translating Dreams into Actions

Believe Dreams are What Success Is Made Of: Successful people catch an idea, refine it and use it productively. They are in tune with their own reactions and realise when an idea is worth pursuing. They know that for a dream to happen it must be backed up with hard work.

Be an Opportunity Spotter: Spot an idea and be prepared to play around with the idea and explore it. At this time you will feel that you have an inner urge to respond and expand new ideas and put them into practice with positive thinking. Activate your success mechanism from within.

How You Think is Often How You Feel: If you think success and start to recognise small achievements, things begin to change. Your attitude to life changes and you see and experience your world in a different way.

Positive Lessons From the "University of Hard Knocks"

No Mistake is Final: Even with new skills you will make some mistakes. No mistake is final unless you make it so. Everything that happens is a learning experience.

Think And Become More Flexible: With newly acquired skills be willing to step out of your comfort zone. You are more competent to make adjustments.

See a New World Emerging: Your world of possibility thinking could be slowly evolving. Instead of instantly recognising the difficulties in a situation you are starting to see the possibilities for growth. Train yourself to see possibilities before you see problems. Be patient with people and go the extra mile.

Obeying An Inner Urge: As you become aware of new possibilities your life is no longer fear controlled. A new freedom helps you to obey this urge that seeks to improve your life. Treat this urge as your friend and it will help you make the right decisions at the right time.

Settle For Nothing But The Best: Believe you deserve the best life has to offer. Be ambitious and aim high; work smarter not harder to achieve your desired result. Also be aware of unrealistic expectations.

Your Most Important Asset is You

Excellence is a willingness to try something new and achieve the best result possible. It is not the end result. Appreciate who you are. Believe in your ability and feel you have been placed in the world for a special purpose. There is no one else exactly the same as you. Learn to respect yourself and do all you can to use this valuable asset to bring happiness to yourself and others. You deserve the best life has to offer.

Crystallise your thinking. Be prepared to examine, explore and clarify your hopes and dreams. Goals are not set in concrete; adjustments must be made along the way where necessary. Believe that truth and knowledge continue to evolve. Be prepared to pay the price for success with hard work and new thinking. Believe the universe is nudging and encouraging you to move forward.

Case Study

Alan's Story

Alan came from a wealthy family and was showered with gifts. Whatever he asked for he received. As he finished high school Alan's world changed. His father's business went into liquidation. His parents separated then divorced, the family home was sold and Alan and his siblings went to live with their mother.

Alan took a cadetship with media advertising. He spent the first month with a company representative and he was then sent out to sell space. He devised a wonderful plan which impressed the sales manager but it did not deliver the goods.

After making the initial contact Alan waited for the business to come to him but nothing happened. He was cautioned by the sales manager that his job was "on the line" if he did not get results. The company felt he had potential and offered to pay for some counselling to help him become sales oriented.

When he presented for counselling he was drinking to excess, behind in car payments, his credit card had reached its limit and he had borrowed $1000 from his mother, which she could not afford. On top of all this he could lose his job. Alan was living in a make-believe world.

Alan was motivated by selfish desire. There was no one else in his world. He had very little concern for family and his siblings. He knew little about listening to the needs of his customers. I explained that some of his false beliefs and values held him back.

Alan's father always came to the rescue when Alan was in a financial crisis. Now there was no "money tree". He was living far beyond his means. Alan was a great salesman if the only thing you had to do was talk. He had been told he had to make a Power Point presentation to help sell the product.

In counselling we discussed the fact that goals and dreams needed to be backed up by a plan of action. Alan needed to change old patterns of thinking. He needed to devise a plan of action, to be internally motivated and prepared to work hard to get results.

He came to realise that to be successful you need to work hard and make the necessary presentations. Alan's plan of action was now more realistic and achievable. He soon realised that wishing alone did not produce results. Alan is now prepared to learn from mistakes.

Alan now believes every new day brings a new beginning with new experiences. He is now working harder and smarter and his attitude about life and others is changing. He is willing to pay the price to achieve his realistic goals. The company is pleased with his progress and new attitude.

Personal Reflections

1. List three short term goals you would like to achieve in the next six months. Put a date beside these goals.

   . . . .

   . . . .

   . . . .

   . . . .

   . . . .

   . . . .

2. List three long term goals you would like to achieve in the next twelve months. Put a date beside these goals.

   . . . .

   . . . .

   . . . .

   . . . .

   . . . .

3. List any problems you might have in achieving your short term or long term goals. Discuss possible solutions.

   . . . .

   . . . .

   . . . .

   . . . .

   . . . .

   . . . .

Action Strategies

You create your own reality – what you believe you can achieve.

Develop a positive attitude – expect the best from life. Persevere and motivate yourself.

Do not measure your ability against others – you are unique in your own right.

Be ready for new goals, dreams and desires – let life surprise you.

Be an optimist – motivate yourself. Be a person of action – not a day dreamer.

Be committed – work smarter, not harder.

Ignite a spark – figure out your goals and go for them.

Live your life around your dream – life needs balance between work and pleasure.

STRATEGY 10

Positive Possibilities - Time to Review Your Progress

Progress Is Made In Small Steps

Congratulations you have reached strategy number ten. As you review your progress you need to realise that you are breaking new ground and that progress is often measured in small steps. You may be struggling with new concepts. Remain open to new thoughts and ideas that are presented. Nobody is born to be either a success or a failure. Successful people step out of their comfort zone and explore unchartered waters.

This is exactly what you are doing now. Living is a challenge filled with purpose and meaning. You are challenging yourself and the way you have lived and are looking for a better way to achieve your dreams and goals.

As you experiment with different approaches to life and learn new ways of relating more effectively, be optimistic. It was Ralph Waldo Emerson who said "Self trust is the first step towards successful living." Trust in the judgements you are making and give yourself a pat on the back for what you have already achieved.

Believe New Approaches Hold Possibilities

As you consider new strategies see how they could fit into your life, perhaps with some modification. If in doubt be prepared to share these insights with family and friends and listen to comments but make up your own mind. You will receive a variety of opinions depending on the persons' attitude to life. This approach is a wonderful way of making real connection with people in your life and to give them some insight into your thinking.

Rewards Come Through Risk

Life rewards effort and success. If a person is willing to change, life has a way of bringing new thoughts that will help. When you look at the spelling of the word life, notice that "if" is in the middle of it. "If" represents the risks you are prepared to take. There are no guarantees that every risk you take will work, but may act as a learning experience. Be prepared to reward yourself, as at least you have been prepared to try.

Practise Makes Perfect

For this program to work you need to absorb new insight into your life. You need to keep up the positive self-talk. When you take responsibility for your life, you begin to make things happen rather than just let things happen. As you practise new skills notice the difference in your behaviour and its effect upon others. You have now put yourself in a position as a seeker after knowledge.

Discovering New Truths

By now it is becoming clearer what you want from life. As you discover new truths, reflect upon them before you make them a part of your way of life.

The most profound changes come from the inside. Your way of thinking, and way of feeling, is changing. As you accept change you become more aware of what you are doing, and why. Think back to where you started and continue to visualise where you want to go.

In life it is quite easy to stray off course. Follow this book as it has been designed to keep you on course and help you to reach your destination. Follow each strategy as they have been intended to help you move towards desirable goals. Do not try to take shortcuts even if you feel that you have a good grasp of a concept being presented. Remember you can learn something new at any time.

Changing Successfully

The aim of the program is to ignite a spark in you to move to the next step in your journey and to give you courage to bring about a successful change, a new sense of freedom to be the person you want to be.

You are starting to learn to value yourself. At this stage begin to put together a workable philosophy that helps you to achieve your new goals and dreams. As you expand your thinking you expand your life.

Change takes courage and determination. Life does not move along in a straight line, there are ups and downs. Once a person recognises that change is necessary for them to move forward they will persist in spite of the difficulties. As you process this material and experience some results the momentum will increase. If others recognise and mention any change they see in you, the process is accelerated. This could be happening to you at this time.

Self Evaluation Rating Scale Number One

We humans are complex, interesting creatures who have a remarkable capacity for learning, given the proper environment and a willingness to be honest with oneself.

Complete the Self Evaluation Rating Scale Number One. Think about how you feel after completing the first ten strategies. Here is an opportunity to honestly review the way you see yourself, your talents and your behaviour patterns. There is no right or wrong way to answer the questions, but answer them honestly describing how you feel at the present time.

Self Evaluation Rating Scale No 1

Evaluate your progress at the end of Strategy 10. Use a scale from one to ten, with one being the least amount of improvement and ten being the greatest. Rate each skill for living. Make appropriate comments as to the progress you have made.

Skills for Living	Very Good	Good	Some Improvement	No Improvement	General Comments
Self Confidence					
Self Assertiveness					
Problem Solving					
Social Skills					
Communication Level					
Listening Skills					
Decision Making					
Attitude to Change					
Positive Thinking					
Work Satisfaction					
Expressing Emotions					
Body Image					
Recreational Activity					
Expressing Love					
Happiness					
Purpose in Living					
Goal Setting					
Discipline in Learning					
Making New Friends					
Progress Evaluation					

Action Strategies

Be gentle with yourself - see each day as a new beginning.

Everything new is hard at first— proceed at your own pace.

Life is a school—lessons are to be learned. life is the best teacher.

Be a calculated risk taker - be willing to try new methods. do not let the past hold you back.

Recognise new life enhancing skills - use them to help you grow.

Strengthen your mind from learning new skills.

Section 2

SUCCESSFUL RELATIONSHIPS

Positive Stress Management

How To Win Friends

Creative Communication

Qualities That Attract

Breaking Out of An Emotional Prison

Innovative Insights

Forgiving and Forgetting

Steps To Lasting Happiness

How To Play The Game of Life

STRATEGY 11

Positive Stress Management– Finding Peace Within

Stress – Friend or Foe

Stress is an everyday fact of life, you cannot avoid it. Stress can be experienced in any change that causes you to make an adjustment. Generally stressful events are thought of as negative such as an injury, illness, loss of job, death of a loved one. Stress can also be positive for example getting a promotion or learning a new skill brings with it the stress of change of status and new responsibility until it is mastered. Falling in love, going out on a first date, joining a social or sporting club brings with it some tension and some level of stress depending upon your temperament.

Stress Comes From Three Sources

The environment bombards you with demands to adjust. You have to cope with interpersonal demands, time pressures, performance standards and other threats to your self esteem.

The second source of stress is physiological or body response. The way you react to problems, demands and dangers is very much influenced by an innate "fight or flight" response. The body responds to anxiety provoking thoughts and events with muscle tension. The tense muscles, in return, increase the feeling of anxiety and stress. The regulatory centres of the brain will tend to overreact and cause elevated blood pressure, tension headaches and can be responsible for heart attacks and stroke.

The third source of stress comes from your thoughts. How you interpret and label your experiences, what you predict for the future can cause either stress or bring peace. Dwelling on your worries causes tension and makes finding a solution more difficult. People who feel that they are born worriers can be candidates for hypertension which can produce health problems.

Progressive Relaxation

A Chicago physician, Dr Hans Selye, developed progressive relaxation therapy, a deep muscle relaxation technique. Deep muscle relaxation reduces physiological tension, pulse rate, blood pressure, and perspiration and respiration levels and helps the body to adjust. This technique has been an effective treatment of muscular tension, anxiety, insomnia, depression, fatigue, irritable bowel, muscle spasms, neck and back pain, high blood pressure, mild phobias, and stuttering.

Progressive relaxation can be practiced while lying on your back or sitting in a chair. Each muscle or muscle group is tensed for five seconds and then there is a short period of relaxation before moving to the next muscle group.

Start with your breathing. Take a deep breath and fill your lungs, hold for a moment and feel the tension and then breathe out, and feel the difference. Frown and notice the muscle in the forehead tighten and then release. Close your eyes tightly, look for tension and then relax them. Keep your eyes closed comfortably. Clench your jaw and then relax. Tense the muscles in your head, your face and jaw, hold for a moment and then relax, and feel the difference. Gradually work your way down your body to your feet and toes. At first only partial relaxation may be experienced, but after practice deeper relaxation will be felt. There are CDs available through pharmacies and book stores that take you through this process step by step.

Meditation

There are various types of meditation – prayer is probably the best known but there is also Transcendental Meditation (TM), mindfulness meditation, and from eastern traditions Zen, Buddhist and Taoist.

All these practices have one thing in common - they all focus on quietening the busy mind. The intention of most of these programs is to direct your concentration to one healing element - one sound, one word, one image, or one's breath as a means to produce a feeling of calm or peace. The aim is to benefit the whole person as it promotes physical relaxation and a deep sense of inner calm. In meditation your brain waves operate at a different level than when awake or asleep.

Meditation is about being, not doing. Sitting still may seem strange at first, particularly if you are usually busy. Time spent in meditation is very beneficial. Everyday thoughts and sounds will still be experienced but meditation helps you to dismiss them more easily because of your relaxed state.

Meditation can easily be practised at home or you can join a meditation class which has many benefits. A simple meditation that you can practise at home, follows.

1. Before you begin this meditation find a place where you will not be disturbed and sit upright in a comfortable chair. Loosen any tight clothing and take a minute to relax.

2. Now begin to focus on your breathing. This is so that you can withdraw from the outside world of thought and turn your attention inward, towards stillness. Become more aware of your breathing each time you inhale and exhale. Once you are aware of your breathing, take slow deep breaths.

3. Keep your attention on your breathing. Withdraw your attention from all thoughts and let your attention become immersed in the feelings of your breathing. Continuously recall your responsiveness to the inhale and exhale of your breath. If you find yourself distracted with thoughts, gently bring your attention back to the feeling of your breathing. With each breath, allow yourself to be in the present for really, it is only the present that exists.

4. Slowly turn your attention inwards and find the stillness in your mind. As you find the silence, be with it. There is no reason to have any thoughts at this time. You have plenty of time all day long to be with thoughts. Now is the time for stillness. Feel the silence and rest in it. If you find yourself distracted with thoughts, place your attention on your breathing again and withdraw from your thoughts. Then slowly turn back towards the silence.

Don't worry if you find yourself thinking a lot. This is normal. Over time, you will gain the ability to quiet yourself more and more. Like anything else, it just takes practice.

If you experience some physical discomfort during the meditation, make the necessary adjustments to bring yourself back to the comfort zone. Just do your best to relax and remain as still as possible during your meditation.

Try practicing this meditation once a day in the evening for about 15 to 20 minutes. Make it a special part of your daily routine.

Affirmations and Visualisations

Social scientist Emily Coue was one of the first to experiment with affirmations. The most famous affirmation was "Everyday in every way I am getting better and better".

An affirmation is a positive statement if repeated on a regular basis day and night will improve the quality of life. It usually takes fourteen to twenty-one days for the affirmation to make a practical impact on your life. Listed below are five affirmations, choose one that is appropriate in your life.

1. I believe what I focus on grows – I now focus on positive thoughts and feelings.
2. I now love myself and others unconditionally.
3. I now choose to be calm and peaceful amidst life's hustle and bustle.
4. I choose to be happy and to enjoy each moment of each day.
5. I believe I am a good person and deserve the best life has to offer.

For affirmations to work in your life visualise the thought being expressed becoming a reality.

Massage

Many healing arts are gaining acceptance today and massage therapy is now looked upon as a useful preventative measure which can be used to relieve tension and stress from the body. A massage relaxes muscles, easing and soothing your aches and pains, but it also rejuvenates and restores balance to the body. The basis of massage is touch. There is increasing medical evidence to show the great value of touch. Touch is so natural that without it people become depressed and irritable.

Emotional release can be felt during the massage or hours after it has ended as massage helps to relax the muscles, stimulate blood flow and remove tension, enabling the body to function more effectively. Massage is not a cure all or panacea for all ills but a way of improving health and for relieving tension.

Healthy Discontent and Inquisitive Questioning

Webster's Dictionary defines curiosity as "careful and anxious to learn". A truly curious person strives not only to find something new but also thinks about how to alter or improve their state of being.

Discontent can be caused by a nudging of God or a higher spiritual power which causes uneasiness and restlessness and a willingness to search for answers. An inner restlessness is not necessarily an indication that you are unhappy, but a realisation that "something" is missing and that you are searching to find what it may be. Take time to stand back and see if you are on the right track to achieve your goals and to experience a deep sense of inner peace.

Addressing Annoying Habits

Annoying habits, like comfortable beds, are easy to get into but hard to get out of. Most people have more good habits than bad ones. Unfortunately, we may be remembered for our bad habits. They often overshadow and can even counteract the good ones. Many of us have spotted habits in us that we would like to change. But often we are at a loss to know how to change them. Sometimes a friend can help point them out to us in a gentle way.

Habits can be changed. You can get rid of a bad habit if you truly are aware of it and want to change. Habits are personal and individual matters. To break an annoying habit or mannerism concentrate on one at a time. If you try to break several bad habits at once your energy and enthusiasm is dissipated and the effect is lost. You could then become discouraged and are likely to give up. When you are successful and have overcome an annoying habit, be prepared to reward yourself. When you exhibit new skills in correcting old habits you weaken the grip the old habits had upon you and change soon becomes evident.

Play and Laughter Reduces Stress Level

Sir William Osler, a Canadian physician, called laughter "the music of life, which makes the unbearable, bearable". Play and laughter are closely related. Make time to enjoy life, enjoy a humorous story, play games, tell jokes to friends, doodle and release the inner child which gets locked up inside of us through tension. Not only does play make you feel good inside, it is also a disinhibitor that opens the door of creativity, an essential element, to help us cope with life's pressures and reduce tension.

Too many people do not know how to play; others limit their recreation to be merely passive observers. There is considerable scientific evidence that the healthy personality is the one who not only plays, but enjoys the game – win or lose. Play is never wasted time. Play and fun make the business of living a more enjoyable experience. It helps to break tension which has built up in a relationship, or when things become so serious that life becomes difficult. Think of play as playfulness where two people become childlike and generate fun, laughter, energy which reduces tension. Playfulness is full of originality, creativity and the only rules it has are the ones you both agree to.

Believe You Are Bigger Than What Happens To You

Know you can relax and rebound from some of life's tension producing situations. You have the ability to bounce back. Everyone has the ability to become an exceptional person in daily living or when facing a major crisis. Exceptional people suffering from a life threatening illness can refuse to be victims. They educate themselves and become specialists in their own care. They demand personhood, dignity and control and do not want to become "a patient number". In face of uncertainty they hang on to hope and still believe in miracles. For these people beliefs are a matter of faith not logic.

Every great achievement in the history of mankind is the ultimate result of some kind of desire. It was the desire to fly like the birds which inspired the Wright Brothers to build the first successful aircraft. Each person is responsible for his evolution and he responds to life's challenges. Accept the fact there will be anxiety and tension along the way but know you can come through difficult times as you tap into positive energy and learn new coping skills.

Energise and Transform Your Life

The quest for peace of mind is universal. Very few are blessed with the internal qualities and external circumstances that automatically assure you of peace of mind. This means striving for a better understanding of ourselves, and using this understanding in developing harmonious relationships which result in less tension. This could be achieved through a willingness to seek assistance from friends or professionals in order to find a better way to solve life's challenges.

Be prepared to shun the "superman image". The superman image comes from a false feeling that you and you alone can save the planet. These people aim for perfection in everything. Admirable as it may be, it is setting yourself up for failure and increased tension in your life. Do the best with what you are good at. Recognise your weaknesses and do not be afraid to ask for help. You cannot achieve the impossible, therefore be kind to yourself and let go of tension producing situations. There is a middle ground, try it by making things easier for yourself and others. See life as a great adventure and be at peace with yourself and your world.

Personal Reflections

1. Identify at least one or more areas of your life where there is noticeable self defeating behaviour which causes you stress.

. . . .

. . . .

. . . .

. . . .

. . . .

. . . .

2. Describe how you deal with stressful issues in your life.

. . . .

. . . .

. . . .

. . . .

. . . .

. . . .

3. Discuss any new way that you have found in this strategy to reduce your stress level.

. . . .

. . . .

. . . .

. . . .

. . . .

Action Strategies

Recognise tension and stress in your life – look at root causes

Believe peace of mind is within your reach if you are willing to make some adjustments and live in the present moment.

Schedule recreation and pleasure into your program – it is essential for good physical and mental health. Escape for a while.

Go easy on yourself and others. Be less critical. Do your best – forget about perfection.

When things are difficult do not be afraid to ask for help.

There is no point in worrying over problems, large or small, which cannot be solved immediately. Put them aside and let them go at least for the present.

STRATEGY 12

How to Win Friends – Building Friendships

To Make a Friend Be a Friend

Making and maintaining great friendships are a challenge for all people but especially difficult if you are shy. Friendship is co-operative and supportive behaviour between two or more people. It involves mutual knowledge, esteem, affection and loyalty. Friends have a deep bond between one another and are willing to offer genuine support. Your genuine friendship can make another person's life worth living. Mean what you say.

Ralph Waldo Emerson said "The only way to have a friend is to be one". Building new friendships takes time and effort. It requires self disclosure, talking and listening, equality and loyalty.

Friends and Acquaintances

Some friendships are made instantly and connection lasts for a lifetime. Other friendships can evolve through regular contact over a period of time. A friendship that is mutually satisfying takes time and energy. Some friendships develop over a long distance and are sustained by a phone call or Christmas card. When these friends meet instant connection is made and there are no gaps in the friendship even after a long period of separation.

There are a number of acquaintances you meet along life's way on a superficial level. Because of life's circumstances you never get to know them. They come into your life and are soon gone. There are some very private people who keep a relationship on a superficial level as they fear getting close in case too much personal information is divulged.

Then there are true friends who wish to get past the superficial and want to know the real person in order to support and encourage.

Try to develop three or four close friends as a support network. Show by your actions that you really care. Demonstrate your sincerity and go the extra mile. Value the time you spend with them. A healthy friendship needs a balance between giving and receiving. Make the best use of the time you share together. In today's world families are often scattered or broken. Learn to build a support system around you that you can truly rely upon in times of need.

Stop Waiting For Things to Happen

Do your part to make things happen so you can reach out and meet more people. Instead of waiting for someone to discover you, be willing to assert yourself and try new activities. Tap into your enthusiasm and energy for living and others will soon recognise you are someone enthusiastic about life and perhaps could be a good friend.

Reach Out To Others

The hunger for friendship begins in childhood and stays with us for the rest of our life. In childhood some individuals may become "loners" and stay this way all through life. When this happens there is just so much of life that is missed. If you feel that you are a loner and want to change, you need to believe that it is possible. It will not happen overnight, but if you work hard enough you can make it happen.

True friends are particularly important because they know your strengths and weaknesses. Friends are valuable to us and give us someone to confide in. Women seem to have deeper and more confiding relationships than men. Most men keep friendships on a superficial level.

Levels of Friendship

Firstly there is the acquaintance level. These are people who you know on a superficial level. You greet them, acknowledge them and "pass the time of day". Then there is the intermediate level where you chat about safe subjects such as the weather, local news, but the relationship may never move past this point. Then there is the meaningful or true friendship which gets past superficialities. These true and trusted friends are a support group you can count on in times of need. They will listen to one another when you are down and share with you when you are on top of the world. They are good listeners and you know that their love and concern for you is there at all times and they will be honest with you.

Make a Tender Connection

You make a genuine connection with others by seeing an opportunity to do a kind deed by acting on the spur of the moment. Thoughtful acts do not go unnoticed. It is these kinds of acts like a phone call, a card for a special event, a thank you note that helps build worthwhile friendships.

It Takes Two to Tango

For a friendship or relationship to blossom it takes two people to work together. A friendship is weakened when only one person is prepared to make all the effort. Eventually this person comes to a realisation or feels that this is not a true friendship and may decide to let it go. Some people are simply takers and give very little in return. Sometimes the giver thinks after a period of time this will change but it is unlikely. Also there are some who give in order to control a relationship. Friendship at times is not easy and can be sorely tested. But if issues are worked through a stronger friendship could develop.

Shining From Within

In developing new friendships shine from within and radiate joy and happiness. Show you bring a loving presence to the relationship and have much to offer.

Maintaining Friendships

Friends are good for you physically, mentally and emotionally. Physically their presence can brighten up your day as you go out with them and enjoy their company. Mentally, friends can be stimulating. It does not mean that they have to agree with you but provide intellectual stimulation. Emotionally it is nice to share your love and concern with a close friend. In a healthy relationship you will feel uplifted by your friends. In a friendship of this kind both people are free to be themselves.

Overcoming Loneliness

To overcome loneliness the first step is to realise you want to do something about it. To feel part of any group there needs to be a level of involvement. Be interested in the activities and slowly make meaningful contact. Step out of your comfort zone and learn something new. This will stimulate your brain, bring about a purpose in your life, and add a new dimension and people will realise you have something worthwhile to contribute.

Social Interaction Skills For Making Friends

Making contact by phone or in person in the first place can be difficult for some — even getting up enough courage to say 'hello'. As difficult as it may be for you, it could even be more difficult for the other person. Introduce yourself and ask questions. This approach helps you to maintain conversation. Most people love to talk about themselves. Life doesn't have to be disappointing and frustrating. The more "hellos" you make the better the chances you have of making new friends.

Acquiring People Skills

The more you understand yourself, your strengths and weaknesses the better you will understand and accept your friends for who they are. No person is ever perfect. Learn to be a soul mate to your partner or close friend by recognising needs, desires, hopes, dreams, and goals. In this way you are truly being in tune with one another.

Rules For Healthy Friendships

Bad Habits Destroy Friendships: Problems in the past need to be discussed. These could relate to taking one another for granted, lack of trust, poor communication, laziness in not addressing problem areas. Recognise what you can do to improve these areas of concern.

Face The Truth: The little things, if not faced, can become major issues and can destroy a good friendship. Aim for truth and honesty by addressing things that cause you concern. Discover the truth about one another's personal needs. Ignore some minor irritating habits.

Recognise What Is Missing: Take time to pinpoint what you believe is missing from your friendship. By having an honest in-depth discussion, it is possible to discern issues. If these are left unaddressed they may fester and bring unhappiness. Recognise the qualities that are good about your friendship.

Avoid Boredom: Step out of a rut. In order to keep an intimate friendship fresh and alive, discover new hopes and dreams. Make space in your life for new activities, both together and separate. Break away from patterns of predictability and find new ways to spend leisure hours. Be open to new ideas that lift the friendship out of a rut. Do not lose touch with the fun, playful and crazy side of your friendship. Engage in activities that are different such as picnics, a walk around your neighbourhood, take a train or ferry ride, visit a museum or art gallery etc. – be less rigid and more adventuresome. It does not need to cost a fortune to enjoy simple pleasures.

Be yourself, Be comfortable: Be comfortable with who you are. Do not be too hard on yourself if you experience setbacks. Value what you are learning about yourself and others. Appreciate one another's differences as they may be complementary and find a way to cope with them. Care for others and at the same time care for yourself.

Accept People For Who They Are

Reach out to those who are a part of your life. Friendship is a two way affair. Both persons must show a willingness to reach out to one another. Accept people for who they are. No one has the right to force change on anyone. You may state clearly things you dislike but it is up to the other person to decide what they will do with the information.

Increase Contentment

Play, laughter and fun are good ways to reduce health costs and to make friends. Smile from the heart. Feeling good inside adds a new dimension to your life and is reflected in vitality and aliveness. We get to decide how empty or full our life will be. Do not let it be empty. Be creative, turn ordinary moments into extraordinary moments with a bit of fun and laughter. It is a wonderful way to make new friends.

Adults laugh about 15 times a day and a four year old about 400 times or more a day. Oh what we can learn from a child.

Enjoy the Present

Unfinished business from the past can stop a person from enjoying the present. Life is a succession of new moments for us to enjoy. Value the moment and make the best of today. Everything that happens in your life can be a learning experience. Each person you meet in life is different. Do not let disappointments from the past hold you back. See each new friendship as a new experience and a new opportunity.

Case Study

Dick's Story

Dick came to counselling as he was desperately lonely and had only one close friend. At the age of 26 he did not know how to make friends. He had gone out with a couple of girls he met through the chat rooms on the Internet. They were nice girls but he was sure they did not like him so he did not telephone them to check.

Dick was a landscape gardener and needed communication skills. He was able to communicate with clients on his work level but when it came to chit chat he was tongue tied and hopeless.

I asked him about school and he said he liked dancing – practising for school formals. He was a good dancer and popular but still painfully shy. I suggested he enrol in a dancing class at an Adult Evening College. He thought that was a great idea.

Prior to joining the dancing course Dick and I engaged in role playing scenarios about meeting new people. He talked about what the other person did — why they liked dancing, interest in music, films, hobbies, holidays and so much more. We also covered similar questions they might ask him. Dialogue eventually flowed freely.

Dick joined Lions — a young people's service group. He also joined a Toastmasters group to help with public speaking. Now he visits a retirement village with a group from Lions and chats with the elderly residents. This has proved to be a valuable contact in learning to relate to people.

Dick had to learn that to make friends you need to be friendly and demonstrate your genuine interest in someone else's world. He now believed if you ask questions you are not prying into another person's world but showing genuine interest. He is now making new friends and enjoys their company. His life has turned around.

Personal Reflections

1. Friendships are an important part of life. What qualities do you look for in a friendship?

. . . .

. . . .

. . . .

. . . .

. . . .

. . . .

2. Describe any difficulties you have in making friends. What can you do to overcome these difficulties?

. . . .

. . . .

. . . .

. . . .

. . . .

. . . .

3. Think of two meaningful friendships. What do you contribute to the friendship and what do you gain?

. . . .

. . . .

. . . .

. . . .

. . . .

Action Strategies

A friendship is a two-way affair – giving and receiving. State clearly your needs.

True friendship takes a lifetime to develop – Do not let the past hold you back.

Thoughtful acts of kindness go a long way – do what you feel you need to do. Communicate freely.

Recognise warning signs when things are not right – focus your spotlight on honesty with yourself and others.

Give freely of yourself – it is the secret of life. Also know your boundaries.

Dealing with differences – no one has the right to force change on anybody. You can say what you dislike.

Acknowledge and appreciate one another's contribution to the friendship.

STRATEGY 13

Creative Communication – Listen, Reflect, Act

Communication is the life blood of relationships. It is impossible not to communicate. Often your manner and voice tone speaks louder than what you actually say. The receiver often does not get the "right" message when there is confused communication. Mixed messages are a barrier to healthy communication. People who are fearful do not communicate with clarity. They do not give a clear message because they are afraid of the consequences of the thoughts expressed. They say one thing but their body reflects something different.

Enjoying One Another's Company

In a busy world make sure there is time to enjoy one another's company. With family and work pressures there is often little time to spend with one another. Do not justify your actions by feeling that quality time is more important than quantity. Maintain a balance as time is a precious gift, use it wisely.

You Never Stop Communicating

Communicate with your eyes as they are considered the windows of the soul. Eyes communicate what is happening deep inside the person. Bright dancing eyes say these people are happy with themselves and their world. Sad, sullen, lifeless eyes indicate that a person is unhappy.

People communicate through words and their body language. Although they are generally not aware of it many people send out non verbal messages using body movements or gestures. This indicates what a person is feeling about what is being expressed.

Recognise Special Moments

Recognise special moments in your relationship when both parties seem to be on the same wavelength. Words are not necessarily verbalised, but you know within your heart this is a special time when your heart and mind blend together.

Aim for Positive Communication

Make your communication encouraging and empowering for those in your life. There are so many things that prevent meaningful communication for partners such as work demands, children's needs, sporting commitments, study and social activities. A major block is television.

There can be so little time left for real meaningful communication after you become involved in all these activities and normal household chores. You are simply too tired. Many couples hunger for a healthy discussion; others use activity to block "deep and meaningful". Such people avoid engaging in meaningful communication. They like to keep discussion on a superficial level to avoid any form of conflict.

Take time to encourage one another at work with meaningful comments that go past the chit chat level. Compliment people who do a good job. Think of ways you can show your appreciation for a job well done. Ask questions which help the other person see that you value and are grateful for who they are and what they do.

A word of encouragement and appreciation can go a long way. Think of the number of people you see on a daily basis and make an effort to brighten their day. Recognise them in some way to let them know they are important.

Hunches, Intuition and Teachable Moments

When you live with a person you get to know them and their mannerisms. When a person has become quiet or has gone into their shell you know there is "something not quite right". Never be afraid to play your hunches, respond to a gut feeling, or an inspirational moment when you feel that you should say something.

These moments may be painful but are tellingly teachable. Often you know it is the right moment to face a problem. You need to obey that inner voice. You simply feel you have no other choice but to confront a situation, recognising at the same time you could be wrong. Discuss issues not personalities. Timing is so important for these discussions. Allow time for a decision to be made after the issue is thoroughly discussed. Listen carefully to what is being said. The presenting problem is not always the real problem. Be brave and grab hold of these moments. The more you respond to them the better your life will become.

All too often the magnificence of individuality is lost under a blanket of conformity. Communicate thoughts and ideas which may make a radical change. Life was designed to be an adventure not a prison. All too many of us lose ourselves in our quest for security.

Listening Is An Art

Modern society is obsessed with what we say, what we wear, how we look and act but not very concerned with the way we listen. Listening is hard work. Women especially want someone who will listen to them, not fix a problem. Men usually want to "fix" things. Here are some simple suggestions:-

1. Give the other person your undivided attention. Give encouragement to proceed by a smile, a nod, or ask a question to indicate your involvement.
2. Paraphrase the material in order to clarify in your mind what has been said.
3. Do not interrupt until the speaker has finished.
4. Be aware of voice tone, body position and eye contact.
5. Check your assumptions about what is being said. It is possible you could be on the wrong track.

Resolving Conflict

It is not what you face in life that counts but how you deal with relevant issues. Do not let unresolved issues simmer under the surface. Rigid beliefs plus the strong need to be right, block true discovery of new insights. Listen to one another; and be prepared to ask for additional information if in doubt.

Simples Rules for Good Communication

Address The Problem Not The Person: Deal with problem areas not personalities.

Listen Before Reacting: Listen without interrupting. Clarify the information by responding to what was said. Acknowledge the point made by the other person. Indicate it is worth thinking about and discussing later.

Life is Often Compromise: Try to develop a win/win approach. This happens when both parties feel they have gained something from the discussion.

Listen To What A Person Is Trying To Say: This means sometimes trying to read between the lines. Ask for clarification to make sure you are on the right track. Some people use the gentle approach and often the communication is not very clear. If you feel a person is attacking you take time to gather information before you respond.

Reach A Solution: Attempt to reach a solution within a reasonable time frame. Give a considered opinion. Ask for time to think about issues. It is very difficult in the heat of the moment to reach the best solution. People have a tendency to think more logically when the pressure is not on them.

Write A Letter: When all else fails, write a letter and leave it to be found when you are not present. This gives the other person time to digest the contents and prepare a written or oral response. Decide on an agreed time for the response. Listen to your inner voice and write from the head and heart. Make it positive. Do not write an accusing letter that could be used in a court of law.

Your Behaviour Speaks

Your attitude to others, your behaviour, your whole body gives out a message before you even speak. Some people who speak loudly and dominate a discussion are often the most insecure. They contradict themselves and their argument is not well thought out. They use force to make a point and do not like to be challenged.

Use your behaviour and understanding of human nature in a manner that encourages those who are shy or reserved to give an opinion. Often the person who is reserved has given a good deal of thought to the subject under discussion and has a valuable contribution to make. In their mind they think no one would be interested in their opinion. Help them to feel important and thank them for their contribution. Also give them the opportunity to remain silent if they wish.

Be aware of contradictory behaviour where you say one thing and do something totally different. This erratic behaviour in communication causes confusion. Be prepared to give reasons why you have changed your thinking.

Secrets of the Power of Persuasion

From time to time you may be in a situation where you wish to persuade a group of people to make a change. It could be a sporting organisation or a working environment or in a personal relationship. Use the psychology of persuasion by convincing others through the logic of reasoning. Be gentle in your approach. As most people are creatures of habit and do not like to be disturbed, the suggestions listed below may be of help to you:-

Make People Feel Important: Be genuinely interested in what people have to say. Treat everyone you meet as the most important person you will meet that day. Ask questions based on the information supplied. Maintain eye contact during the discussion. Create an atmosphere of safety and trust so that even more information may be forthcoming. Use your own creative thought process, based on your intuition, to lift the level of communication. Pass genuine compliments when the other person responds with new insights.

Create Interest & Benefit For the Other Person: Make your approach of interest and benefit to the other person and there is an instant win/win situation. When you want to persuade someone to do something, create a point of interest that attracts attention and instantly the person sees benefit for himself.

Encourage Good Questions: If you start to gain support for an idea encourage people to ask questions of you. Commence your reply so that it soon becomes evident that the question asked is worthwhile. This helps to take some of the tension out of a deliberation. In order for a person to feel persuaded to act in a certain way there must be an opportunity for discussion and compromise.

Present Possibilities: In order to achieve a good result, present several possibilities for consideration. You are offering a number of different approaches to show the listener that you are open and looking for the best way to achieve the best results. Encourage other possibilities to also be listed for consideration. Make the task "our task".

Be Flexible: Increase your level of flexibility in your discussions. Show you are willing to change your thinking pattern as new information is presented.

Suggest A Trial Period: In the art of gentle persuasion if there is an agreement in principle decide on a trial period that is to be reviewed on a certain date. Others who are involved then feel that they have a chance to try the suggestion and still have power to reject/amend the idea when the trial period is finished. This reduces tension in implementing new procedures in an organisation.

Personal Reflections

1. On a rating scale of one to ten, rate yourself on your communication skills

   Listening: . . . .

   Communication: . . . .

   Assertiveness: . . . .

   Problem Solving: . . . .

2. Think about three things you would like to discuss with your partner in more detail.

   . . . .

   . . . .

   . . . .

   . . . .

   . . . .

   . . . .

   . . . .

3. Describe how your communication skills could be improved.

   . . . .

   . . . .

   . . . .

   . . . .

   . . . .

   . . . .

Action Strategies

Become a clear communicator - and communicate clearly your thoughts.

Listen for what is behind the words - look for the real meaning.

Communicate both from the heart and brain - put your true feeling into what you say.

Respect others' beliefs and opinions - listen to what others say.

Stop talking, start listening— clarify information, stop being defensive.

Look for the best in people - you find what you look for.

Little acts of kindness go a long way—be thoughtful and considerate. Welcome opinions different to yours.

Value feedback - listen to what others say and think about you. Analyse what is said and take any appropriate action.

Build the win/win approach into your negotiations.

STRATEGY 14

Qualities That Attract – Desirable Qualities

Equality

A healthy relationship needs respect where individuals are free to be themselves and to express their opinions. At times couples will have differing opinions which need to be respected and listened to. In a relationship you do not have to be in agreement on everything as life is a series of compromises. Each person brings to a relationship values, beliefs and standards that are important to them.

Respect

Respect in a relationship is expressed by encouragement, passing genuine compliments, never taking each other for granted and being able to listen to work related problems without the other person trying to solve the problem. It is a way of sharing and getting "something off your chest". You need to be able to freely express your concerns.

Good Sense of Humour

People with a good sense of humour soon find people attracted to them. They know how to tell a story tastefully that does not offend and at the same time do not dominate a conversation. These people know when to be serious, funny or to say nothing but be fully present.

Perhaps you have become too serious and need to release the "clown" within. You have forgotten how to play but can learn lessons from children around you. Be fun to live with. Introduce the surprise element into your relationship. Tease a little in a harmless way.

Physical Attraction

Physical attraction plays an important part in making an initial contact with a person of the opposite sex. Beauty is in the eye of the beholder. There is much more to a relationship than sexual chemistry, it is more than a spark of love or lust that attracts people to one another.

Everybody is sexual. It is part of our journey from birth to death. There is no right or wrong way to express your sexuality just your way. Sexuality can be a potentially positive, joyous and enriching experience based in part on physical attraction.

Trademark – Self Awareness, Self Acceptance

Develop your own trademark which helps you stand out from the rest of humanity. Blend together awareness of self, strengths, weaknesses and total acceptance of others. Believe in your own individuality and uniqueness that helps you to stand out.

Success Attracts Success

Those who are successful in life attract people with similar ideals. Success, for many people comes through hard work. They invest their time and money wisely and are proud of their accomplishments.

Say What You Mean

Communicate your changing needs throughout a relationship and listen to those of your partner. Remember that your partner will not know what you need unless you express it. A person may think they know what you need but are never quite sure. Make time for meaningful conversation which gets past the chit chat level. See this time as quality time and an opportunity for relationship growth.

Sharing Feelings

The journey towards togetherness, true intimacy, is never ending. It is time to let go of hindering attitudes and embrace new ones. You need to develop a greater awareness of your feelings, both positive and negative, and express them freely.

To achieve emotional closeness you need to create a positive, healthy, joyful and stimulating relationship. The process can be slow. You need to get to know one another on all levels. If anger is a problem, do something about it. Enrol in a course on anger management or seek professional help. You need to know what you are feeling and why you feel. Know when you are ready for a committed meaningful relationship.

Be Romantic

Romantics have a way of reaching the soul of their mates with the use of words, poems, flowers and little gifts which express love.

People still like to be romanced. Stop hiding your romantic side because you feel too embarrassed. We are often too silent about things that matter. It is time to release your long buried passion for romance.

Show your appreciation for acts of kindness. Let the other person know how these acts affect you. It turns mundane love into something magical as you explore romance.

Show You Care

It is often the little things that you do for one another in a caring and sensitive manner that really counts. People who are caring and sensitive show it by their actions. It is often the people who make a lot of noise that people are really attracted to. But often this type of person does not relate well in a committed relationship as they can be selfish and self centred. In this highly sophisticated world people are very discerning and know what they want or do not want. They are often more cautious as they grow older or if they have been through a divorce.

People who care about others often reflect this in the way they care about themselves and their possessions. These people have learned an important lesson in life, that is, you cannot fully love anyone unless you love yourself. If you respect yourself and your property it is very likely you will respect others and their property.

Assertiveness Not Aggressiveness

Become a person who is able to assert themselves in situations without becoming aggressive. Assertive people say what they think very clearly and know what they want from life and are not prepared to be pushed around or manipulated.

Often these assertive people are leaders in their field and offer a stimulating relationship. Just as they are passionate about life and work they put the same intensity of passion into a relationship. These people have a mind of their own and know how to assert it. They also respect others and do not ride "slip shod" over them.

Some men and women find it hard to deal with assertive personalities as they see them as a threat. Assertive people present ideas for discussion in a logical manner backed up by rational thought and are prepared to listen to others with an open mind.

Togetherness and Separateness

Many people do everything together. It may suit them to belong to the same groups, sporting and cultural activities. However, for many, there needs to be a balance between separateness and togetherness. Personal space based on trust and time to be alone can enrich a relationship. People then have a variety of interests to share with their partner and also there is an opportunity to make new friends.

Independence and Interdependence

In a relationship people admire those who are independent and can stand on their own two feet. They are people in their own right and do not need a relationship in order to survive. They are also willing to be interdependent but recognise there must be a healthy balance.

When people are totally dependent on one another and do everything together they could eventually feel a sense of being smothered and there is no time for personal privacy in the relationship. Do not set yourself up for failure by expressing a sense of possessiveness. Most people do not want to be possessed or controlled. Where there is trust in a relationship there is a true sense of freedom.

Possessiveness is a sign of insecurity. It controls and cripples a relationship and stifles freedom for growth. To maintain a healthy balance between independence, interdependence and possessiveness, issues need to be addressed openly and honestly, and people need to have the freedom to be who they are.

Social Skills, Common Courtesies and Commitment

Social skills help a person feel comfortable in interaction with others. These are an acquired skill. Some people are good at encouraging others to share and are genuinely interested in what they have to say. There are some people in life who are gregarious and outgoing and have little difficulty with social skills while others are tongue tied, shy and lack social skills.

Learn to be generous and outgoing as you share yourself and your possessions with others. Build boundaries that let others know where they stand and how far you are willing to share your generosity. Do not use money to buy friendships. People will take advantage of this and you will learn the hard way that a fool and his money are soon parted. Learn from others. Read on the subject or enrol in a personal development course.

Manners and common courtesies play an important part in a relationship. These niceties are important to men as well as women. With the rise of the Women's Movement many men are confused about their role and what they should do. At all times do what you believe is correct according to your belief system and ask your partner for feedback. Remember it is the little things like common courtesies and social skills that can either make or break relationships

The Commitment Phobic

There are people around who are afraid of a committed relationship. These people want to "play the field" and have a good time without responsibility to anyone else, as they like their single life. There are single people who enjoy their freedom and do not wish to be locked into a committed relationship. In some cases they are afraid of being hurt.

Re-educate Yourself

If you feel confused about relationships seek professional help. Read about or enrol in an adult education course in interpersonal relationships and learn from class interaction. Recognise any weakness in relationships and do all you can to correct them. Invest time and money in learning about relationship interaction.

Case Study

Terry's Story

Terry was 40 years old. He had been divorced for three years. His ex-wife had custody of their two children aged eight and ten. Terry was confused about the dating scene. Things had changed so much that he felt he needed help.

The majority of women Terry met were extremely independent. When he went to open the car door he was rebuked. If he asked a woman to go to dinner, they often insisted on paying for their meal. To his utter surprise some women made it quite clear that all they wanted was sex without any commitment.

For him, in the last 20 years the dating scene had changed. Many women were more assertive and wanted equality in relationships. Two of the women he dated told him he was not ready for another relationship. Terry had much to learn about relationships.

When Terry came for counselling he was still very fragile and had not accepted any responsibility for the break-up of his marriage. Terry was very confused about why his wife left. He was in a hurry to find another woman as a replacement for his ex-wife. He believed he wanted another woman like his previous wife but who would be faithful.

It soon became evident in counselling that he did very little to support his wife during his marriage. He belonged to a soccer club and he trained for two nights a week. He played soccer on Saturday and often met with the boys on Sunday for a barbecue at the club. He was "married" to the club. His wife stopped going to see him play and was not involved in the Sunday barbecue as she had the responsibility of the children.

At night he helped his children with their homework but did very little around the home. He had never asked his wife the cause of the break-up. Terry was a "man's man" and very proud of it. He knew very little about women especially their physical and emotional needs. He also knew very little about himself.

When Terry was asked what qualities he looked for in a woman all he could think of was a good "homebody", someone who liked sex and was good with money. I then approached the issue of love, romance, intimacy and feelings. Terry was lost and said they were never discussed. They did not discuss their sexual relationship but simply did it. This whole area of intimacy was new to Terry. On several occasions his wife complained that he never told her he loved her. Terry told her she was silly and needed to grow up.

When asked what he thought women wanted in a man, he replied a good worker, someone who loves children and who keeps the yard tidy. He never had thought much about relationships. Counselling is still continuing.

Personal Reflections

1. List in order of preference qualities you look for in a partner.

Qualities	Male Preference Rating	Female Preference Rating
Honesty		
Good Communicator and Listener		
Sense of Humour		
Generous Nature		
Responsible with Money		
Love of Children		
Physical Attractiveness		
Shows Love and Affection		
Sexual Enjoyment		
Believes in Relationship Equality		
Positive Thinker		
Good Decision Maker		

2. Now discuss four of the most important qualities you have selected and why they are important to you.

. . . .

. . . .

3. Discuss four qualities you feel you bring to a relationship.

. . . .

. . . .

. . . .

Action Strategies

People who are passionate about life put a smile on their face and a twinkle in their eyes and are noticed.

Have courage to be yourself – live your personal creed.

Develop a good sense of humour— do not treat life too seriously.

Own and accept your achievements – be a person who wants to be successful.

Be a person who is a good lover, communicator and generous in all aspects of life.

Be prepared to make a commitment – people need to know where a relationship is headed.

Show appreciation – never take a person for granted. Pass genuine compliments.

Be less judgemental – look for the best in each person you meet. No relationship is ever perfect.

STRATEGY 15

Breaking Out Of Your Emotional Prison

Get In Touch With Your Emotions

People often suppress their real feelings, positive or negative. The psychological term is “containment”. Conversation is maintained on a safe plane with very little emotional content. These people are stuck in rigid belief patterns that they have setup in order to protect themselves from further hurt. They actually feel that they are emotional cripples and their emotions will get them into trouble. They feel wretched and underneath hate what they do or fail to do but feel that this is the only way they can cope. If you were told as a child men do not cry, you need to understand that in today’s world some of this thinking has changed. Both men and women are encouraged to express feelings freely. Suppressed emotions may surface at inappropriate times as irrational behaviour.

Emotions of all kinds, including jealousy, envy, greed, need to be expressed. There will be times when it is appropriate to show displeasure and times to be loving and joyous when things are going well. Study people around you who are positive and yet freely express a full spectrum of their emotions. Whatever these people are feeling at a given time they will express. If they are unhappy it will soon be clear in the behaviour expressed.

Time To Remove Your Mask

Perhaps it is time to stop pretending, or playing games and to remove the mask you hide behind to protect your true self and feelings. Some people find self disclosure to be a threatening experience. They may even feel that if they remove their mask and let people see the real person you may not like what you see. Self disclosure is the only way for an authentic relationship to grow and for trust to be established. When this happens adjustments to behaviour may be necessary.

Some see removing the mask as risk taking behaviour and a threat to a relationship, but it is in fact a way to really connect and understand another human being. We all have so much to learn about one another. For feelings to flow freely you must be in touch with your true self.

Blend Thinking and Feeling Together

Feelings reveal in some way the intensity of your thinking. If you are feeling wretched within it will soon show on the outside. If you feel that your life is falling apart it will be reflected by the way you react to life's difficulties. At this stage you may wish to untangle your feelings and express them fully. Negative undercurrents can cause feelings to be unclear and decisions difficult to make.

You now need to ask what happens when you attach a thought to a feeling? You are labelling, describing, defining, interpreting or judging the feeling. Our beliefs, which are our deep feeling experiences, are responsible for the quality of our lives. As you change your beliefs, you change your behaviour. It is the feeling behind the thought that gives it power.

There is no limit to what we think and feel. Ideally life can be a liberating experience where thoughts and feelings are freely expressed. When natural feelings, both positive and negative, flow freely in a relationship there is a solid base on which to build.

Feelings Enrich a Relationship

Positive and negative feelings enrich a relationship. When any range of feelings are repressed you do not know exactly what the other person is thinking and feeling. Feelings are not good or bad but indicate a person's reaction to a given situation.

To overcome problems you need to rebuild trust through respect and total acceptance of the other person. As trust and love are built into a relationship self disclosure may start to flow naturally because both parties feel secure based on a strong bond of trust, love and acceptance.

Positive Feelings

Love: This is a powerful positive force that can enrich your life. It is a healthy emotion that helps you to love yourself and others. When this happens you have a positive approach to the world around you.

Happiness: This is a matter of choice. I can choose to be happy or choose to be sad. Life is not always easy but the key is found in how you react to life's challenges. Happiness can be felt as a result of an achievement that helps the individual to feel pleased and contented with the outcome. It also can result from peace of mind. Even in a difficult situation you can be happy with the way you cope.

Joy: A person who is a joy to meet is a person who has found joy and happiness and radiates this feeling to others. Joy for these people is not based on possessions but the way they feel about life.

Hope: This is a powerful positive emotion which inspires people to keep trying in spite of all the difficulties surrounding them. Hope encourages a person to have an “I can do it” attitude.

Negative Feelings

Fear: This emotion is like a cancer of the personality and helps to paralyse the person from reacting in any manner. To overcome fear you need to face it and do something to overcome it. Fear drains positive energy from the body. Fear can have a positive effect when it prevents you from doing something that can cause danger or hurt.

Anger: Anger, frustration and hostility show when you are displeased with a situation and react negatively. Often when this happens an individual feels challenged and takes a defensive attitude. Healthy anger happens when you express your displeasure with a situation and make positive constructive suggestions to improve it.

Worry: Some people believe they are “born worriers” and are fearful and anxious. Worry sets up a vicious cycle as it does not go anywhere. Fear and worry are closely linked. Worry achieves nothing and does not help to improve the situation but causes more anxiety and confused thinking. It drains energy from the body and a person feels empty and powerless.

Worthlessness: People with poor self esteem feel worthless, useless, and no good to themselves and anyone else. They have built up a great sense of rejection by society, through loneliness and feeling abandoned believe no one really cares. These people need to find some way to change their thinking pattern and to see that they still have something worthwhile to contribute.

Mood-swings: Mood swings are caused through the need to make a decision, small or large, at a time when the energy level is low. Become aware how your mood-swings can affect your feelings.

Know when you are out of sorts. Be attentive to what is going on in your life. When at war with others there is no peace within. When you feel tired, listless, and lethargic and are not in the mood to do anything it could be that your positive emotional energy is being blocked. If mood-swings persist they can lead to depression, and it is important to seek professional help.

Honest Thoughts and Feelings

Positive and negative thoughts flow through your mind daily. How you perceive thoughts and what you do with them is all about your attitude to yourself and life. Your life will be shaped by the thoughts you think and how you feel. Strong positive attitudes cause positive responses and accelerate growth and learning. You and you alone are responsible for the way you express your feelings. Be prepared to express whatever feelings are coming to the surface once you can identify them. Healthy, natural feelings, both positive and negative should flow freely in a relationship.

Feelings Produces Awareness

You can live your life any way you choose. If you choose positive inspiration or aliveness you will express a full range of emotions. Evaluate, judge, analyse and interpret all your behaviour patterns to see if they will help you to achieve your goals.

Everything you attract into your life is based on the feeling this is what you deserve. The more you believe in yourself and self worth the more willing you are to share your feeling needs with others. Now is the time to clean up your thinking and convince yourself that you deserve the best life has to offer. Really come alive and enjoy each day for what it brings. Welcome all your feelings and freely express them.

Case Study

Ken's Story

Ken came to counselling after his wife Thelma threatened to leave him. He thought he had the best marriage in Sydney. Ken and Thelma had been married for six years and they had two children, a beautiful home, a car and money in the bank. Ken had a successful plumbing business.

Thelma told Ken that their life was cold and empty and lacked expressions of feelings. Ken was confused as they had regular sex, initiated by him. He helped with work around the home, did the shopping, looked after the children. He asked what else he could do.

Like many other men he did "things" and displayed very little positive loving feeling gestures. He never told Thelma he loved her, thinking she would know this by his actions. Ken thought this is the way Australian men behaved. This is what he had heard at the hotel. He then discussed the fact that his father never expressed loving feelings to his children. His parents' marriage broke up but he never knew why. His parents had found other partners and remarried and appeared to be very happy.

Ken decided to meet his Dad for a couple of beers and to have a "man to man chat". His Dad told Ken that he had been an idiot by not expressing love to his family. This conversation made an impact upon Ken as he could see he was "a chip off the old block".

He started talking freely and openly to Thelma for the first time in their relationship. Thelma was exceptionally angry about the way Ken had treated her. She gave no guarantee she would stay in the marriage even if Ken went to counselling. This really upset Ken.

Ken began to express a wide spectrum of his emotions — positive and negative. He wrote a letter to Thelma apologising for his behaviour which she destroyed in anger. Now, Ken is so different with his children and keeps telling them they are precious and that he loves them dearly. Prior to this time, Ken, like his dad, was preoccupied with work.

Thelma came to one counselling session. At this time she had developed a new relationship. Within two weeks Thelma had moved out of the family home with their two children. Ken was devastated but realised he could do little but accept the situation.

He saw the children on a weekly basis and developed a good relationship with them. After three months in counselling Ken joined a "Divorce Recovery Group". He started to make new friends with men and women and was not in a hurry to find another relationship. He realised he needed to change and understand more about interpersonal relationships and that he was not ready for another relationship.

Personal Reflections

1. On your rating scale how well do you express the full spectrum of your feelings?

   Positive Feelings

   1 2 3 4 5 6 7 8 9 10

   Negative Feelings

   1 2 3 4 5 6 7 8 9 10

2. Discuss how feelings affect your relationship and what you can do to improve things.

   . . . .

   . . . .

   . . . .

   . . . .

   . . . .

   . . . .

   . . . .

3. Describe what you have discovered about yourself and how you express your feelings.

   . . . .

   . . . .

   . . . .

   . . . .

   . . . .

   . . . .

Action Strategies

Remove emotional blocks – It is time to stop stifling your emotions.

Be in touch with positive and negative emotions – be able to express them freely.

Remove your mask – stop hiding your feelings. Let people see the authentic you.

Feelings influence thoughts, be aware of them.

Let your light shine – express your feelings freely. Be sensitive to the feelings of others and how they react.

Believe how you think and feel shapes your life.

STRATEGY 16

Innovative Insights For Living & Relating

The Road to Success Is Always Under Construction

Every day you learn something new about yourself and about life. There comes an acceptance that no one is perfect. There are things that you may need to discard from your life and lessons you may need to learn. Recognise that you are a fragile human being, under construction. At this time in your life there are many new learning experiences.

Life is made up of pain, sadness, happiness and pleasure and in between states. When there is pain and sadness ask yourself "What can I learn from the experience and what could I have done differently?"

When you experience joy, happiness and pleasure let it linger so you can enjoy the full impact in your life. The joyful experiences help to act as a cushion for the tough blows that come your way.

Let go of the need to be right. As you travel along life's highways and byways be prepared to say you are sorry especially when it becomes evident you have simply made a mistake and in the process hurt someone. Be gracious in the manner you express your apology.

Learn From Others

You can learn much from your fellow travellers in the journey of life. I accept the Buddhist teaching "That everyone who comes into your life is a teacher". A person may teach you a valuable lesson that will enrich your life, or you may see something in that person that you dislike and recognise this quality in your self which needs to be addressed.

People are very interesting. Many have put their lives together in a way that brings them satisfaction. Watch the way others share significant information. Study people and watch how they express themselves with their eyes, face and the way they use their body.

Notice the way these people are interested in others and remember names and significant events. See how people balance the level of attention on themselves, but also involve others.

Never be afraid to ask another person a question or take a conversation to a deeper level. Show in practical ways how you care about others by following up a discussion with a phone call or remembering a special event like a birthday or death of a loved one. Be sensitive to the needs of others.

You learn about relationships from those around you. You also learn about fashion and the way people wear clothes in a distinctive manner. Notice their colour combinations. What you can learn from others is endless. Let people see you are warm and approachable. Express genuine interest in what they say and do.

Put Yourself Into What You Do

To make a real connection with others you need to believe in yourself and what you do and what you say. Words need to be backed up by actions. People recognise when there is genuine interest in their wellbeing.

Give the best you have to life and you will find in most cases life gives you back far more. Try to be the best you can at what you do. Be open and flexible. Become aware of life's important lessons.

Freely express yourself. Let people see the real you. Respect other people who may have ideas that differ from yours. Enjoy and express your light heartedness. Laugh, have fun and even be a little mischievous. Recognise issues in your life which need to be addressed to increase your performance rating at work, at home and with friends.

Be Passionate

Be excited and enthusiastic about all that life offers. Become passionate about some aspect of your life. Explore it and enjoy finding out more about your passion. It could be a hobby, sport, your work, or something you would like to understand better. When you are enthusiastic about a certain aspect of your life you will feel full of energy.

Be passionate about life and those things that excite you. Allow the passion to develop your skills and feel you have something worthwhile to offer. Passionate people welcome new information as they have an open mind and welcome challenges.

Be Creative

Innovative insights help you to use your creativity and imagination. This helps to turn ordinary events into extra ordinary events. Being creative and imaginative does not have to be expensive. A warm welcoming smile with a few balloons and streamers around a room can quickly change the atmosphere. People start to feel chatty, happy and are soon smiling. All it takes is a little effort and some imagination to add a new dimension to your social life.

Some people have a natural creative flair. This is evident in dress style, home décor and in the way they relate to others with spontaneity and naturalness. Such people love the surprise factor in life and are not thrown into frenzy. The spontaneous person is very adaptable and enjoys life's fun experiences.

Do not be afraid to experiment with your creativity as it can add another dimension to your life. When creativity is expressed life feels alive and exciting. There is a new sense of openness as you approach a part of your life that may have been ignored. Stand out from the crowd by your innovative approach to life.

Creativity is not only linked to art, drawing, writing, poetry. Creativity can be linked to all aspects of life. A creative person asks how to do things differently. This could relate to photography, gardening, a hobby, interior decorating, your style of cooking, the way you dress, the way you express yourself in interpersonal relationships. Creativity frees up the individual to be true to self. It is a way of drawing attention to yourself that is acceptable and natural. You become regarded as a person with a flair for living.

Appreciate The Wonderment of Life

One of the wonderful discoveries about life is to capture its wonderment. We live in a beautiful world and we need to stop and appreciate the splendour of nature. There is just so much we take for granted each day. It is often only after we lose something precious that we start to appreciate how beautiful it was. The world is full of interesting people who collectively are making some wonderful discoveries. Appreciate the beauty and wonderment of each moment of each day. Even if life is tough take time to see and experience some natural beauty.

Add A New Dimension To Your Life

You know from past experience that playing safe does not get you anywhere. Within each of us there is a yearning to be creative and to be different but often we do not know where to begin.

Curiosity, wonderment, adventure and creativity helps you to look at life differently - to explore, risk and investigate new ways of doing things. It is turning ordinary moments into extraordinary moments. It is really living in the present and appreciating the wonder and beauty around us. Curiosity of the mind brings about adventure and new dimensions for living. Discover new ways of doing things. Break your normal routine and find something new to explore. Create some rituals which add to the enjoyment of life. It may be a ritual that each Friday you celebrate the end of a working week and the beginning of a weekend. It could be something you do on a Sunday that is rewarding. Rituals have a meaning of their own. A candle on the table can mean that this is a special meal.

Recognise Your Own Inner Critic

Often people are their own worst enemy. Time and time again they disappoint and hurt themselves by their attitude. When something happens, big or small, their first reaction is often a negative one. This type of person is never happy unless they have something to complain about. During their journey through life they have developed a mentality that says that they are not good enough. Therefore they live out this script and keep putting themselves down. They are in no way innovative or creative.

It is like having an inner saboteur. Instead of expecting that they will do their best to face life's challenges, they give up and feel life is against them and they cannot win. When challenged these people are ready with excuses because they believe whatever they do it will not work out to their advantage. They are creatures of habit bogged down in negativity.

They are full of negative tapes from the past. Reinforced messages of fear and insecurity from the past still run their life today. It is deeply ingrained in the psyche. They act out what they believe about themselves. It is only through awareness and insight into this behaviour that a person can come to understand what they are doing to themselves. The only way transformation can take place is by the person taking personal responsibility and being willing to face change. This can be a crucial time in their development as they recognise their inner critic is destroying any happiness.

Start with little things about you that annoy you and others and correct them. Notice the difference in life when these irritations are corrected. This gives you courage to attempt to discover other strategies to resolve negative approaches to life.

The inner critic can prevent you from enjoying life. Silence this aspect of life by finding new skills that stop you from punishing and putting yourself down. Recognise now is the time to find a new approach to living. There is a lot of catching up to do as you no longer listen to the inner critic.

To control your inner saboteur build on your positive attributes. Through critical appraisal recognise what you are good at and become better. When you receive compliments from people accept them graciously and feel you have worked hard and deserve the praise. This helps you to be less critical of aspects of your life where you are not as proficient. When you are unsuccessful, instantly remember the times when you were successful and you will feel less frustrated.

Solitude is a Valuable Asset

Solitude helps to recharge our batteries and to be at peace with our self and our world. It helps you to cope with an insecure world with its pain and disappointment. It improves your quality of life as people are drawn to you and see there is a special quality which they would like to discover. Solitude is a powerful tool for daily living and it helps you to apply innovative insight which could enrich your life.

Pamper Yourself

In life, many people have a tendency not to listen to their body until it breaks down. People push themselves very hard and mistreat their bodies by what they eat and drink. Even when tired they continue to push until they are forced to stop. In society today there are some major advances in this area. Let us now look at some of the best ways to pamper your body:-

Massage: The body responds to a therapeutic massage

Relaxation and Rest: The body needs at least seven hours of uninterrupted sleep to cope with the normal pressures of life. A relaxation tape can do much to achieve a good night's rest if sleeping is a problem.

Hot Bath or Spa: If you have a large bath or spa it is good for relaxing the body. A bath or a spa can also be a good place for meaningful communication. Subdued lighting and soft soothing music can add to the atmosphere.

Sensible Activity: A regular walking or exercise program at least three times a week can help the body to function effectively. You walk at your own comfortable pace and know how far you need to walk.

Medical Check: Each twelve months visit your doctor for an annual check up. Prevention is far better than cure.

Dare To Be Different

Be an innovative leader in your field. It doesn't matter how old or young you are. Be a somebody and not a nobody. Dare to step outside of your comfort zone and be willing to help to build a better world. Think of something you have wanted to do all your life but have never done. Go out and do it, if that is what you really want. Look at the way you dress. Be willing to review your wardrobe and consider making some changes. Dress in colours that can bring attention to you and help give your personality a lift. Try a new hairstyle or a colour which will improve your appearance. Have a real purpose in your life and really, really live it. Break free from the labels society puts on people. Be a person in your own right. Be innovative in your approach to life. Believe you can make a difference.

Learn to be inventive with yourself in some way. It could be that you are a good story teller and you gain a reputation for this talent. Allow your personality to come through and show that you are a person who cares and can be trusted. You then become a person who others confide in. Develop a hobby that is perhaps a little unusual which could be of interest to others. If you build innovative thinking into your life things can change. It is well worth trying.

Case Study

Charmaine's Story

Bill and Charmaine had been married for 10 years. They appeared to be a happy suburban couple with two children, nice home and car, good holidays. Bill worked for a manufacturing company as a production engineer. His boss, the production manager, was very demanding and was never satisfied.

Charmaine was working as a personal assistant three days a week. She recognised their marriage was in trouble; she was terribly unhappy as she felt the spark had gone out of the relationship. Their sex life was non existent. Charmaine suggested counselling to her husband Bill who strongly objected. He had been brought up in a home where no one discussed personal issues. He was flat out coping with work and did not need extra stress.

Charmaine went to counselling much against Bill's will. When she returned, Bill did not enquire about what happened. He thought much about the situation for a week and then asked for the counsellor's phone number.

To Bill's surprise the interview went very well. Bill discussed his work and it so happened that it had been a tough day; Bill talked non stop for 20 minutes. I asked Bill what he planned to do with the work problem. Bill suggested he could talk it over with his wife and then decide on a course of action.

At the next interview Bill felt it was time to bring the work situation to a head and he would meet with the managing director. At the meeting Bill offered to resign which was not accepted. The director interviewed Bill's manager who told a different story from his perspective. The director decided to employ an independent arbitrator to handle the issue. The manager was annoyed with this approach and told the director he had let him down and resigned on the spot. The director tried to persuade the manager to rethink the drastic action but to no avail. The manager gathered up his personal possessions and gave Bill a piece of his mind in front of all the employees.

Within 24 hours the director offered Bill the job of production manager, he readily accepted with a substantial increase in salary. Bill's old manager rang up two days later and asked for his job back but it was too late.

Now there was still the problem of sharing personal issues in the relationship. Bill on his own initiative decided to enrol in a communication course which would help him at home and at work.

Bill now is the one who discusses issues at home and wants to know how Charmaine is feeling. His level of self awareness has reached new heights and he now shares his own personal needs. He has a different relationship in the factory with the staff. He is interested in them as people and has become a good listener to their needs. In Bill's words "The stress level has been reduced by 60% and the whole atmosphere in the factory has changed".

Bill is now working in counselling with Charmaine as they explore sex, love, and intimacy. He is not afraid to ask questions or to admit freely where he is lacking.

Personal Reflections

1. Discuss any new insights you are learning about yourself and your life style

. . . .

. . . .

. . . .

2. Name three people in your life. Describe two of their best characteristics.

Person	Characteristic
	1. 2.
	1. 2.
	1. 2.

3. As a scholar in human nature what are you learning from people, yourself and life?

. . . .

. . . .

. . . .

Action Strategies

Explore positive possibilities – see new ways to approach life.

Dare to be true to yourself—listen to your gut instincts. play your hunches.

Be your best at what you do – put effort into what you do at home and work.

Bring to life your unexpressed side – be fun to live with.

Reconnect with self and others – stop running away from yourself and others. change relating pattern.

React positively to life's obstacles – look for the best even in the toughest times.

Come out of the maze – believe there must be a better way to organise yourself and be prepared to find it.

Recharge your batteries – take time for peace, solitude and reflection.

Catch up on living – stop existing, start living. Improve your lifestyle. Be innovative and creative.

STRATEGY 17

Forgiving And Forgetting – Letting Go Of The Past

Forgive Yourself And Others

If you are going to move forward in life you need to be less judgmental of yourself and others. There is no sense in holding onto pain and hurt from the past. All this does is to make you unhappy and to distance yourself from others. You can become fixated on the past and want to get "even" with the person or persons who you believe may have hurt you.

In other situations it is often harder to forgive yourself than it is to forgive others. At times you are harder on yourself and want to keep punishing yourself. This achieves nothing other than to make the problem more complex. You may become bitter which can result in extreme loneliness.

When you are prepared to forgive yourself and others you are willing to let go of the past and move beyond blame. Instead of wallowing in self pity, move on with life and turn mistakes and disappointments into stepping stones to a new life.

Learn From The Past and Free Yourself

To forgive yourself means accepting the fact you are not perfect and will make mistakes. Take time to feel the impact from the past and accept responsibility. During this time see what you can learn, so you do not make the same mistake again. Feel the pain and hurt but be prepared to move on to a new phase of life.

Life's Ups and Downs

The roadway of life has its bumps, obstacles, mountains and detours. Then there are the plateaus, the free flowing rivers, the peak experiences and the grassy plains. These all combine to enrich our journey. Unfortunately life has no signposts. You eventually recognise that you are on the wrong road when your life is full of unhappiness. You know you need to take a different route and try a different approach to life. When you are down the pain is often too hard to bear and you feel that you are a victim of unfair circumstances. At this time you feel tied up in knots. There is an internal struggle that is taking place and you may become angry and illogical which only hurts you. Try to untangle your confusion as the struggle is to no avail.

Life's Mysteries

Life is a mystery and strikes some cruel blows to you personally as well as a nation. Some of life's events are hard to fathom. When a nation goes to war it is a mystery why one person is killed in action and his mate beside him survives. Some events are beyond human explanation.

Even as you try to recap events from the past the internal struggles do not seem to ease. You may even become more confused. It is only when you allow love and forgiveness to flow that the pain becomes more bearable. You realise that for life to flow freely again you need to make some adjustments to your thinking and forgive yourself and others. This at times is not easy to do and often needs a superhuman effort,

Putting Life's Puzzle Together

Remain open to new learning experiences. Do not see a setback as something from which you will never recover. With faith in yourself believe you can adjust and put pieces of life together in a new way. This will allow you to move on. Believe you will not be defeated. Be determined to keep searching until you find the missing pieces.

Saying Goodbye to Guilt

Feeling guilt ridden, results in a "cancer" of the personality. When you feel guilt-ridden everything seems negative. People shrivel up and die inside. It is a cancer that eats away at your positive thoughts and life becomes fear controlled.

Forgiveness, for some, means doing all that you can to make amends for a wrongful act. It is being able to say you are sorry and really mean it. Being unforgiving hurts you more than anyone else.

When you feel that you have been hurt unjustly and believe you cannot do anything about it, leave the matter with the judicial system. Do not feel that you can take retribution into your own hands.

For many, faith and belief in a loving and forgiving God helps to wipe the slate clean and to begin again. By holding on to grudges you are limiting your life in the present. Replaying your injuries helps you to be attached to the past. Experience an inner positive power to rise to this occasion and make a fresh start with major adjustments. Forgiveness is like a miracle that frees you from the past.

Learning to Say No and Not Feel Guilty

You may feel imposed upon by others. Some people take, but give very little back and do not show much appreciation for your help. There comes a time when you need to stand up for yourself and say "no" and not feel guilty. Some feel if they do this the other person will not like them and they will lose the friendship. Stop and reflect and discover that if you take a stand it could improve the relationship or it could come to an end.

When you value your self esteem you start to see how unhealthy some relationships have become. It may come as a surprise to the other person when you challenge the relationship. Your reaction may pull them up in their tracks and help them to realise what they are doing. On the other hand they may wish to terminate the relationship. Whatever the outcome, believe you have learned an important lesson about standing up for yourself without being aggressive.

Learn to listen to positive self talk that gives you courage to assert yourself in a new way. Instead of filling your mind with self limiting thoughts explore new ways of expressing yourself. Maybe for some time you have been telling yourself there must be a better way to live; believe this self talk and start asserting yourself today.

Bad Things Do Happen To Good People

Life is not always fair. There are things that happen to us that simply defy explanation. You may have every right to feel angry about what has happened to you. Your pride may be hurt and you feel that you are simply an innocent bystander. You keep asking yourself "why me". There are no simple answers. Do not develop a "poor me" or "victim mentality". Be prepared to get on with the job of living. Try to see all sides of the problem and how they may have arisen, without laying blame. This may call for changes to be made and you may need new skills to reach a better outcome. Make each experience a learning experience and let go the anger.

Becoming a Better Not Bitter Person

The disappointments of life have an effect upon you. They can make you a better person or a bitter person. It all depends upon your attitude to life. No one escapes life's disappointments.

We think we know what we need to make us happy but when our plans are upset we react. At times life knows what is best for us even better than we do. When our plans become suddenly interrupted and we are forced to take a different direction it can be distressing. At times disappointments cause major upheavals and other times minor ones, which affect us in some way.

To become a better person you need to learn to make adjustments. Feel the full impact of the pain and hurt, at the same time, allow the healing process to begin. Pick up the pieces and start to move forward.

It is not easy to pick up the pieces and start afresh. If you remain bogged down your health will suffer, you will become miserable and dejected, feeling there is nothing worth looking forward to and depression could become a major factor in your life. Through the power of forgiveness do all you can to cancel past debts? When this happens you experience the healing power that true forgiveness brings.

Admit When You Are Wrong

When something goes wrong in life, first question yourself. Being able to state that you were wrong in a situation and to be able to say 'sorry' is very difficult for some people. For such people pride gets in the way and they see an acknowledgement as a sign of weakness. People respect others who are able to acknowledge that they have made a mistake. But if there is no acknowledgement the hurt may fester.

Do not bluff your way through life. Learn to admit to yourself and others when you are wrong. This builds a bridge of acceptance and others gain an insight into the real person. You feel better and have nothing to hide. This creates within you a feeling of peacefulness and can be a valuable learning experience.

Learn From Your Mistakes

To learn from your mistakes you need to stop and analyse them. Do not run away from them without learning some of life's valuable lessons. Take time to do some serious introspection. Ask yourself "What could I have done that would have had a different outcome?" "What warning signs along the way did I fail to heed?" "How could I have been better prepared?" "What lessons can I learn from this failure?" These and other questions help you to learn from life's mistakes so that you can move ahead realising that you will be careful not to make the same mistake again. Unfortunately some people are slow learners. The person who never makes a mistake often does very little with their life. Hindsight is very valuable but unfortunately you cannot live your life backwards. Listen to the teacher within. Do not let the past hold you back from enjoying the present. The past is gone and all you can do is to learn from the mistakes.

Forgiving The Unforgivable

Forgiveness is not something to be taken lightly. There is a real depth to forgiveness and it takes a lot of courage. Be attentive to what is going on in your life. Know what needs to be forgiven to make a fresh start. Do not seek justification for your actions. Be honest with yourself.

Forgiveness can be expressed in words and reflected by actions but it needs to be felt in the heart. You then realise that you have learned much about yourself and life.

Pain, anger, hurt and frustration from the past is released through forgiveness and you can be at peace with yourself. You no longer hold resentment or a grudge or desire to punish yourself. Using your inner strength to let go the experience and get on with the job of living.

Add A New Dimension To Life

Forgiveness is a powerful force to free you from the past. Everyone has regrets for some of the things they may have done in the past. Do not let the past haunt you and stop you from enjoying the present. Forgiveness can provide for you a spiritual awakening that leads you to explore more fully this dimension of life that may have been neglected.

Broken Hearts Do Mend

It takes time for broken hearts and lives to mend and for forgiveness to be felt. Heart and mind needs to be ready for forgiveness. Our inner environment helps us to express and receive forgiveness. With the passage of time, support by good friends and with willingness and determination you decide not to be crushed by things you cannot change. Your body is a powerful machine designed by the Master Architect and has the power to heal itself. Feel that you are now ready to let go of the past, the pain, hurt, and the disappointment, the sadness and all the other emotions you associate with the experience. Be assured that you will recover from the experience and you can become a happier and better person.

Case Study

Fiona's Story

Fiona arrived in Australia from Ireland on a working holiday and met Jack. Prior to leaving Ireland her parents made her promise two things — (1) she would attend mass regularly (2) return to Ireland in the next 12 months and settle down.

The relationship with Jack really took off and within three months they were living together. She had now stopped going to mass. After about eight months Jack proposed to Fiona and she accepted. Within a week she had become seriously depressed as she had not told her parents about Jack. She decided to seek help with this problem.

Fiona's parents had strong religious convictions and Jack had never realised how important mass was to Fiona. It had never been discussed in the relationship. He suggested they find a church and attend.

Jack at this time had no contact with her parents and decided to rectify the matter.

He suggested that they invite her parents to Australia for a holiday and he even offered to pay their fares. In the last 12 months he had started his own export-import business and it was doing exceptionally well.

The parents agreed to come to Australia but wanted to be independent by paying their own fare. Jack and Fiona still did not tell her parents about their engagement. They decided to keep this news a close secret until they arrived in Sydney. Then Jack would ask the parents permission to marry Fiona.

Fiona made plans to marry in Dublin. She was now happy and contented and free from all guilt and fear.

Personal Reflections

1. How do you cope with the statement "learn to say no and not feel guilty?"

   . . . .

   . . . .

   . . . .

   . . . .

   . . . .

2. Are you able to practise the forgiving and forgetting experience or do you still hold grudges. Share your thoughts.

   . . . .

   . . . .

   . . . .

   . . . .

   . . . .

   . . . .

3. How do you apply the principles of forgiveness in your relationship?

   . . . .

   . . . .

   . . . .

   . . . .

   . . . .

   . . . .

Action Strategies

Live in the here and now—forgive yourself and others. Stop punishing yourself.

Be prepared to accept an apology from a person who is sincerely sorry.

Let go of grudges – stop wanting to punish others.

Stop blaming others – heal from within. Do what you can to make amends.

Replace outdated attitudes – guilt is destructive like a cancer of the personality.

Understand you are not perfect – you are a human being with strengths and weaknesses. Sometimes you fail yourself and others.

It takes faith to say goodbye to guilt – faith in yourself and in a "power greater than yourself."

STRATEGY 18

Steps To Lasting Happiness

Happiness Is A Personal Responsibility

Many people go through life searching for happiness which seems to elude them. It is not people or things which make you happy. You are responsible for your own happiness or unhappiness. What you get from others is an added bonus. Happiness, contentment and joy are all interrelated. It is simply being able to appreciate your accomplishments and learn from your mistakes. It is learning to live in the moment and enjoy life. It is also seeing an opportunity in life to bring happiness to someone else who is less fortunate than you.

Finding True Happiness

This life of ours may soon be over. It is not a dress rehearsal it is the real thing. Do not put things off until a seemingly more appropriate time. Live your life in the way that you feel is right. Each person is responsible for the way he lives his life.

The way ahead may not be clear. Finding your way in the dark can be extremely painful. If you persevere you will see a ray of hope. Love, value and make the most of your life. Life does not always meet our demands. Make a commitment to yourself as you are making a fresh start that whatever happens you will make the most of each situation. Life at times could be rough but face it with courage and determination.

Life has a way to give you signs to indicate you are on the right track or not. It could be in something that happens to you, the remark of a friend, an article you read or a thought you follow. Watch for indicators to help you see clearly which path is right for you. Do not get bogged down in past behaviour patterns. Make sure the door to the past is permanently closed and your new life is evolving. Visualise possible positive outcomes. See the new direction your life is taking.

Believe you deserve the very best life can offer. What you expect is usually what happens when you do your part to give the best you can to others. Life has a wonderful way to reward you.

Wake up and live your life in a way that will bring joy and happiness to yourself and others. True happiness is expressed in good times as well as in difficult times. True happiness is not artificial. It comes through many of life's experiences. It is a genuine quality – an expression of the heart. It is not only saying the words but freely displaying your happiness by your actions.

Clear Negative Thoughts

Your thoughts reflect your belief. If you want to change the way you experience life you must be prepared to change your beliefs. Your thoughts, your environment and what makes you feel good enhance the beauty of your life and help you to discover happiness. What you focus on grows. If you expect to be unhappy it will surely follow because that is the way you have conditioned yourself to believe. Now is time to change your thinking and believe you deserve the best life has to offer. Replace negative attitudes with positive thoughts that can bring happiness.

Do not let life drag you down. Believe you can overcome life's setbacks. It all depends upon your way of thinking and your attitude to life. Thinking differently is the first step.

Happiness Can Be Elusive

When you experience a degree of happiness take time to enjoy and appreciate the happiness moment, however fleeting it may be. Life never goes along in a straight line, as there are ups and downs. When you start to savour happiness the bumps are not as painful. It may appear that you are unhappy because of what has happened but believe eventually things will change and happiness will reappear in your life.

By taking control of your mental programming you are able to convince yourself that what is happening is only a temporary set back and that happiness will come your way again. You learn to ride the storm and cultivate an inner stillness to help you through it. All you are doing is replacing negative thoughts with a new positive perspective. This way you learn to turn adversity into an advantage.

Appreciate Your Life

Do not just sit back and expect life to happen. It is up to you to go out and make things happen. If you just wait around and see what life brings to you, the result may be very disappointing. As you travel through the unchartered waters of life, recognise each day is yours to live, grow and enjoy in spite of what happens to you. Remember to count your blessings no matter what, and do not allow the problems to overwhelm you. Life needs a balanced approach. See each stage of life as a stepping stone. Appreciate the fact that you are alive and still have hope in your heart.

Learn From Happy People

Happy and contented people are not free from pain and sadness. These happy people have an attitude that helps them make the best out of every situation. Each day they look for the best in themselves and in others. Happy people attract happy people. They are a joy to be with as they express positive thoughts which often lead to a stimulating discussion. These people radiate enthusiasm for living. They are often warm hearted and generous people who give freely of themselves. What helps these happy people to stand out is that they are not afraid of failure. They know that they have the resilience to bounce back from life's cruel blows. With an optimistic approach to life and a clear head they have found the secret to happiness.

Believe Life Can Be Different

It does not matter what state you are in, life can be different. Have you ever wondered why so many apparently successful people do not appear to be happy? For one reason or another these people are so busy achieving that they have forgotten how to be happy. There is an inner restlessness that pushes them further but they do not take time to enjoy and appreciate their achievements. Life truly rewards action but take time to enjoy your achievements. Some people are happier travelling to their destination than arriving. These people enjoy the challenges and the journey. Feel happy about the contribution you can make to life.

To bring about change in your life you need to believe that your life can be different if you want it to be. Happiness is not just for a few people it is available to all who will embrace the happiness habit. Most people do not want a dreary predictable life. If you are one of these people it is time to come out of your shell and believe you are ready to follow a new approach to life and open a new doorway to happiness.

Living Joyfully

We find joy, peace and happiness as we accept each situation in life for what it is. Make the best out of your disappointments or your successes. It is all in your attitude to life.

Your inner core or belief system helps you to enjoy each day for what it is and not what we want it to be. Joy and happiness are the result of being contented. It is a state of mind which helps you to appreciate life. At the same time if you believe it could be better look at ways to change the outcome. It is a feeling that you are in tune with life and life is in tune with you. It helps you to give freely of yourself to others and there is now a deep sense of purpose and meaning that leads to happiness.

Seven Keys To Lasting Happiness

1. Be happy with your own company. Welcome family and friends.

2. Look for an opportunity to do an act of kindness or show encouragement to someone else. Be happy for someone else who has been successful.

3. Enjoy the company of people in your own age bracket. Welcome people older and younger.

4. Discover what makes you happy and enjoy this activity on a regular basis. Reward yourself.

5. Be open to new discoveries, e.g. hobbies, sport, cultural or new learning experiences that provides a challenge but at the same time bring inner happiness.

6. Think about things you can do with other people and activities you can do alone which bring happiness to you and others. Be adventuresome.

7. Happiness does not always involve spending money. Some beautiful, happy, peaceful moments are free for you to enjoy such as a walk along a beach, a stroll in a park, a beautiful sunset, watching children play or people passing by.

Be Happy

Be convinced that with a new attitude, happiness is within your reach. It may be necessary to make some adjustments in your thinking. It is time to clear out the old thinking and bring in the new. Action is vital.

Be prepared to follow your deepest instincts, thoughts and hunches in your search for happiness. Remember a kind word or deed goes a long way. Be patient with yourself and others. We cannot expect to change old thoughts and behaviours in a day or a week. It has taken a long time to get to the point where we feel bogged down in self pity and negative thinking. With courage and determination things can change and happiness can become a reality.

Personal Reflections

1. On a rating scale 1 to 10 (10 being the highest), how do you rate your level of happiness. How did you reach your decision?

   Happiness Level . . . .

   Comment . . . .

   . . . .

   . . . .

   . . . .

2. Name three things you do that make you feel happy and why?

   . . . .

   . . . .

   . . . .

   . . . .

   . . . .

3. If you are unhappy state the cause of your unhappiness. What immediate action can you take to improve your situation?

   . . . .

   . . . .

   . . . .

   . . . .

   . . . .

   . . . .

Action Strategies

Happiness is for everyone.

Believe you are responsible for your happiness.

Accept that at times happiness can be elusive.

Recognise that thoughts reflect your beliefs.

Believe there is a better way to live.

Reach out to others.

Learn about happiness from happy people.

Appreciate what you have.

STRATEGY 19

How to Play the Game of Life and Win

Life Does Not Come with An Instruction Book

All the games you play come with a set of rules. Life, however, does not come with a manual. For efficient functioning mankind has established laws, ethics and morals. These guidelines may change as you gain new insights. Life is a not a dress rehearsal so you need to enjoy what it offers and live each moment. Life is what you make it – it is for living, learning and loving.

To get the most out of life you need to know what you want from life. If you spend most of your time engaged in frivolous activity there could be little lasting satisfaction. Look at people around you and learn from them. Have a balanced approach between work and play.

The Road of Life Can Be Bumpy

The road of life is very similar to travelling on unsealed roads in the outback. When you strike a road full of pot holes and corrugations you simply slow down. To be able to roll with the punches of life and to bounce back you need to slow down and reassess the situation. Getting back to the analogy of the unsealed road, if it gets too rough you may need to pull out your map and look for an alternative route. When the problems seem never ending, stop and see what you can do differently. This shows a willingness to accept some responsibility for what is happening. It also helps you to reconnect with energy and intellect necessary to make a wise decision. Decisions made on the spur of the moment based upon what we feel alone will often be regretted.

The bumpy road of life can be simply an indicator to tell us we are on the wrong track. It also could be the way that life is teaching you some important lessons. When we learn these lessons, the journey could become smoother.

Life is unpredictable. We may feel in control of a situation and suddenly life changes. Life for many is short. Do not let anyone talk you out of enjoying life your way providing it is not destructive to your mental or physical health or those around you. Some people may be jealous of your success and resent your achievements. Make the best of life with the resources you have at your disposal. Have reasonable expectations.

Life's Disruptions

If you are feeling that you do not know what to do next, take time out, and do nothing until you are able to think more clearly. In the midst of disappointment and sadness, take time to see what you can learn from such an experience. Your loss could relate to the death of a loved one, a marriage breakdown, a business failure, or some deep seated hurt you are trying to come to grips with.

Believe no one owes you anything as you are responsible for making things happen. Expect good things to happen through hard work, perseverance, and persistence despite the bumps or the potholes. If you are not successful in your first attempt be prepared to try again. Life is a testing ground to take you to new heights. Some people give up when they are faced with setbacks. The best lessons of life are learned in tough times.

How To Enjoy The Game of Life

Try to think of life as a game. To enjoy any game requires a clear understanding of the rules. Set up rules or convictions you hold true and live by them as they help you to establish boundaries. It also requires a clear intention to support those around you. You do not need to be an Olympic athlete in pursuit of a gold medal to be successful. Success in life is often made through small achievements. You start by feeling the fear and know you are going to give the project all you have to make it a success. No one can require more from you than this commitment. Along the way support yourself with positive messages of encouragement.

Preparing to play soccer by buying a book on golf is not helpful. The reason many people do not enjoy a high quality of life is because they are not certain about the rules. No matter how wonderful life might seem at any level, the possibility for improvement always exists. At the same time, if something is running well there is no need for adjustments. To enjoy the game of life be aware of your needs and those around you. Decide what brings you joy and pleasure and make these activities a part of your life.

Forget About Trying to be Perfect

Accept the fact that you make mistakes. The person who never makes a mistake is the person who does not step out of his comfort zone. Learn from your mistakes. Be careful not to repeat the same mistake again. Feel good about yourself and what you have achieved. Accept yourself for who you are with all your imperfections and know you can change and be better.

You may feel that there is not much freedom for you as you feel trapped and manipulated. Take time to look for an opportunity for you to regain your inner strength. Make the best of each experience for what it is. Simplify your life. Clear away complexities that confuse. Do not resent what others achieve in their life.

See Life As A Creative Playground

See your life as a creative playground. Have you noticed children in a playground and how excited they become - they just want to run from one activity to another as they see new games to explore. You can learn a lot from children and capture some of their excitement about life.

Be open and willing to try new things in every aspect of your life. Enter the creative playground of life with a strong intent that you are going to enjoy it. Who really cares how good or bad you do. It is mainly your pride that gets in the way and you feel shy and embarrassed. The main thing to remember is that you are willing to try and this is part of the great Aussie tradition.

Play, laughter and fun are a good way to reduce health costs. Play allows you to free up the body and at least for some time you can forget some of your worries. Let yourself go, get out of control, have a good belly laugh, and do something non adult like. Build into your life a variety of experiences that produce a balance between work and play.

Playfulness As a Priority

Play is a healing therapeutic force which helps to relieve temporarily some of the pain and hurt you may have been experiencing. Make cheerfulness and playfulness a high-priority in your life.

Human beings are often fragile. Bodies can be easily damaged by illness, accidents and wars. Hearts can be broken, minds wasted. A little bit of play and laughter can go a long way to help with the healing process and to get your life back on track.

Improving Your Environment

Some people are hoarders of papers and "stuff". There is hardly anywhere to move when you visit the home. Your environment is often symbolical of the way you think. Thoughts and ideas need to be clarified in your mind so that you can clearly see where you are heading.

Decide to de-clutter your working environment and clear away things that are not essential. If you are not prepared to throw them away, put them out of sight. Have a good cleanout of your home, especially the bedroom, your yard and other areas that need attention. Sort out what is important and let go of the rest. If this task looks too big ask friends for help.

When all this happens you will discover a new lease of life. Consider replacing some of the "old stuff" with an updated version. You will feel better and be more productive.

Know What Is Important

Take time to reflect upon what is important to you. If you are going to de-clutter your life you need to be clear about what you are ready to let go and what you want to keep. You can listen to thoughts that are expressed by others but you have to make the final decision. The changes you make could be the difference between success and failure.

Thoroughly explore opportunities and possibilities. Look and expect to see opportunity where others are afraid to. See your life more clearly and the direction you are heading.

Value each experience that comes your way and recognise what needs to be changed. Be dedicated in your search for truth about yourself and about life. Develop a positive mentality that helps you cope with life's experiences. Take time to "spring clean" the negative and draining thoughts that sap away your energy and vitality.

Expanding Your Thinking – Enjoy The Game

Appreciate What You Have: Focus on what you have, not what you do not have. Do not make comparison with others around you.

Forgive and Forget: Set yourself free from the past. We all make mistakes. Be prepared to say you are sorry.

Create Opportunities: Be an instigator and make things happen.

Be Courageous, Believe In What You Have To Say: Do what you believe is right for you. Do not be held back by the opinions of others.

Be a Somebody: Believe in flashes of inspiration. Believe you have something worthwhile to contribute to life however small the contribution may be. Look for opportunities to show acts of kindness. Act like a winner.

Act Out Of Conviction: You are not here to rescue people. You are here to support and encourage others to see problems more clearly so they can then make better decisions.

Put Excuses Behind You: Be a doer and not a 'gunna'. Stop making excuses. Decide the best time to make important decisions.

Let Go of The Past - Live In The Present

Make the best of each minute of each day. Find enjoyment in what you are doing, however mundane it may seem to be. Find a way to turn your life into something a little more exciting. Think about some minor changes you could make. You have no guarantees that there will be a tomorrow so you need to learn to live in the here and now and make the best of it.

A New Set Of Rules To Win The Game Of Life

1. Live by the Golden Rule "Do unto others as you would have them do unto you".
2. Develop a win/win approach to the battles of life.
3. Expect the best from life and put your best into what you do.
4. Never give up on learning – keep mind and brain stimulated.
5. Develop a balanced approach between work and pleasure. Enjoy your journey, for some people work is pleasure.
6. Become aware of games other people play but do not be manipulated.
7. See life as a series of "now" moments. Enjoy each moment and learn from them.
8. Develop an "inner knowing"; head and heart working together.
9. Forget about perfection - aim for improvement. Be a doer and not a "gunna".
10. Believe everything you do matters. Be accountable for all your actions.

Case Study

Betty's Story

Betty was a senior stylist at a leading hairdressing salon. She was very good at her work but was absolutely hopeless in relationships with men. At the age of 24 Betty decided she needed help with this problem. Betty had a younger sister, her father was an alcoholic and her mother was shy.

At work she had power and controlled a staff of four. Her clients loved her and she was popular. She was a good stylist, a good manager of staff and listened carefully to clients. She changed her approach when in a relationship and tried to fit into what the other person wanted. Decisions on where to go were difficult and she pushed them back onto her partner. Her partner often drank to excess but she never confronted him. She never said no to sex even if she did not want it. Relationships usually ended within four weeks.

In counselling Betty said that her mother was always afraid that her husband would leave and so she fitted into his life.

There were two important questions Betty needed to face. Firstly, what she had to offer in a relationship and secondly what she wanted from a relationship. Betty found both questions extremely difficult. She decided to think about these questions prior to the next interview.

Betty arrived at the next interview quite excited. She had asked a number of her clients these questions and got some interesting replies. Betty said I want to give of myself, my love, my encouragement, help others and in general to make the most of life. Then she discussed what she wanted was love, acceptance, equality, romance, fun, good sex, honest communication and the list kept coming.

It was suggested Betty do an assertiveness course to which she readily agreed. She is now exploring what she needs in a relationship. Fear is being replaced with positive thinking.

Personal Reflections

1. As you play the game of life do you believe you play the game honestly?

   . . . .

   . . . .

2. Describe the set of rules you use to play the game of life.

   . . . .

   . . . .

   . . . .

   . . . .

   . . . .

3. Describe how, where and when you have fun as you enjoy the game of life.

   . . . .

   . . . .

   . . . .

   . . . .

4. To find fulfilment, enjoyment, what adjustments do you need to make?

   . . . .

   . . . .

   . . . .

   . . . .

   . . . .

Action Strategies

You make your own rules – understand yourself and respect others. Rules need to be honest and fair and based upon ethical and moral standards of society.

What you look for you usually find – look for the best in others.

Be passionate – expect the best.

Develop a sense of humour – Do not take yourself too seriously.

Drop defences – let people see the real you.

Be a player not a spectator.

Know what really matters and make it a criteria for living.

STRATEGY 20

Follow Head and Heart - Review Your Progress

You Have Come A Long Way – Designing a New Life

It is now time to pause and reflect and review your progress. Perhaps you have never been able to complete anything very much in life so applaud yourself for the guts and determination you have demonstrated. There could now be a new shift in your perception as how you see yourself and life. Thoughts and ideas which you have considered unrealistic could be making sense. New life-changing ideas are already impacting upon your life.

Breaking Free of Self Sabotaging Patterns

You may now feel less negative than when you commenced this book. If so the 'inner saboteur' is being controlled. You have become less critical of yourself and are feeling stronger as you get a new lease on life.

You may be noticing changes in your thinking. You could be changing your attitude to life's challenges. You realise that now you have the power to choose the way you live.

Changes you are making could benefit everyone. You are not on a selfish pursuit. Knowledge gained can have a wide-reaching effect. Change brings about release from some outdated ideas you held about life. Accept yourself a little more every day. Make each day count. See your life changing.

Positive Acknowledgment

Give yourself credit for the changes you have made. You are now learning to handle life much better. Realise that a setback is not the end of the world. Simply regroup your inner resources, learn from the experience and proceed again.

You are learning to expand your mind. You need to apply new knowledge or you will lose it. You may feel unsure as you assimilate this knowledge and apply it in your life.

There is a clear identification and acceptance of positive values that can enrich your life. Put these positive values to the test and see how they work for you. Identify these new strengths and let them become part of you. Allow things to happen at their own pace.

Recognise how you can benefit from the information you have gleaned. Be open to wonderful surprises and discoveries you are making at this time. What you get out of life depends upon the effort you put into it.

Touching The Wisdom Within

The concepts expressed may seem to make a lot of commonsense as you will now realise what works for you and what does not work. As you draw upon the wisdom from within, your ability to discern what is right for you becomes clearer.

Difficulties may also be more evident. You may be even more willing to discuss these issues openly with a friend or an independent counsellor. Be open in your discussion. It is time to be honest with yourself and others.

Unstoppable Momentum

Recognise that your desire for new learning is developing. You are being carried along with new knowledge, new energy and new concepts for living. Discard things that no longer fit in your life. You are now replacing things of the past with positive new concepts to enrich your life. You now recognise you do not want to stay the way you have been for so many years.

Now by using a creative, constructive approach to life you can make important decisions more readily. Each moment of each day has become precious as you are open to these new learning experiences. Keep focused on what is happening now.

You now have moved beyond some of your difficulties. Notice that where you once were blocked you have found a new freedom to overcome difficulties. You are stepping towards your future life. You can now do what needs to be done to achieve hopes, dreams and goals. You can see things more clearly with a new found confidence.

Inner Assurance

It may not be completely clear what is happening but you realise now that life is changing. This could be the new emerging true self, the person you were meant to be. Be patient with the progress you are making. Be open to life changing experiences. Deep down you know that these life changing experiences will enrich your life. Welcome these new changes in your life and treat them as your friends to encourage you on life's way. You now know without a goal there is no direction.

Soak up new experiences and apply them in your life. Do not be afraid at this time to delve deeper into your life in order to understand your motives. Experiment, trust your intuition, and see where it takes you.

Feeling Good About Yourself

As your self esteem and self confidence grows you no longer fear what might happen if you do decide to make some major changes in your life. You now believe more in yourself and your ability. You are accountable for your decisions and take full responsibility for them.

If you believe that you are on the right track, do not let anything hold you back. Believe there is no such thing as failure but simply learning experiences. Stretch yourself. Feel your dreams are now within reach.

Events often unfold according to your expectations. You can now see the way progress is being made. You like what you are discovering. You are changing thoughts about yourself and life.

When you feel good about yourself you have a healthy attitude to others. At this time people could be noticing something different about you. You also recognise and accept there are still problems waiting to be solved. Divide your problems into two groupings, the difficult, and the not so difficult. Tackle the not so difficult ones first and see the results. Feeling good encourages you to continue to move forward. When you act from head and heart, solutions begin to appear.

Feeling Secure Within

Security in an uncertain world is found within the individual. Money does not bring security but it can help you cope effectively with some of the challenges. Life has prepared you for this period.

If you have been a good student, learning from life's lessons you will move forward in your life's journey. Setbacks, detours, uncertain times do not last forever. The cycles of life keep changing.

Your current thinking may appear to be the ultimate truth, until experience teaches you otherwise. Rigid thinking blocks true discovery. We hang on to so much stuff that has little use for us today. It is a time to de-clutter your life.

Putting Together Life's Puzzle

You may find it hard, at times, to fit all the pieces of life's puzzles together. Yes, there are pieces that seem to fit together, but often the plan of life is not clear as parts of the puzzle seem to be missing. Remember there are ten more strategies to come. Be patient.

All people, whether we realise it or not, are searching for the meaning of life. During your lifetime you will explore many new pathways. Some will have some new truths. You will know within yourself what is right for you. You know from knowledge and new learning how to be strong in a world that has become very insecure. New discoveries are a part of living.

Self Evaluation Rating Scale No 2

Place a tick in the appropriate box as you evaluate your progress. Do not be too hard on yourself but be honest. Compare Self Evaluation Rating Scales No 1, 2 and 3.

Skills for Living	Very Good	Good	Some Improvement	No Improvement	General Comments
Self Confidence					
Self Assertiveness					
Problem Solving					
Social Skills					
Communication Level					
Listening Skills					
Decision Making					
Attitude to Change					
Positive Thinking					
Work Satisfaction					
Expressing Emotions					
Body Image					
Recreational Activity					
Expressing Love					
Happiness					
Purpose in Living					
Goal Setting					
Discipline in Learning					
Making New Friends					
Progress Evaluation					
Notes to Myself					

Action Strategies

Growth is breaking new ground – life is what you make it. Go the extra mile. Brainstorm all the possibilities.

Learn to make the best of each moment – leave your ruts. Enjoy each experience for what it is – good or not so good.

Become aware of what is happening – events unfold according to your expectation. Live in a state of excited anticipation. Experience life with freshness and clarity.

Become self-inspired – believe in yourself and your new found ability. Success is the result of good judgement and hard work.

Like what you are discovering – if it makes sense, believe it. It will help you to discover your true potential.

Section 3

SUCCESSFUL LOVING

Let Us Talk About Love

Love and Actions Go Together

Romance – A Way Adults Play

Exploring Intimacy

Sensuality

Rethinking Sexuality

STRATEGY 21

Exploring Intimacy – Building Togetherness

Let Us Define True Intimacy

The word intimacy means "into me see". Intimacy occurs when a connection is made with another human being on a deep level. For self disclosure to happen, a person needs to be open and willing to trust the other person. It means taking down your walls, letting the other person see the real you with your strengths and weaknesses.

Creative Intimacy

All of us are creative. We have a creative mechanism in us that if developed can add another dimension to life blending creativity and imagination. To think creatively we must rise above intellectual thought and be able to think outside the square. The mind is an invisible computer with infinite power, it is a creative masterpiece. Creative intimacy is to be found within the individual. Life's riches are within the mind so take time to be still and tap into your creative intimacy.

Intimacy with oneself is a basic requirement for relationship growth. Intimacy requires courage to explore oneself. It is a way of relating whereby each person within a relationship finds support, enhances his or her potential and at the same time respects each other's uniqueness. It establishes a bond of togetherness.

Creative intimacy is an unending process of discovery and growth. It involves a process of separate and mutual nourishment. The more we nourish and care for ourselves the more we have to give to others. Intimacy is an attitude, a way of being, and relating to others with closeness, trust and connectedness.

Barriers to Intimacy

The Private Person: Some people are proud of their reputation and will not allow another person to get close to them. They are afraid of closeness.

Fear of Self Disclosure: When trust is betrayed, confidence broken and information leaked to others, a barrier is set up. It takes time for trust to be re-established.

Childhood Conditioning: For some, it was ingrained in childhood, that you do not tell others anything that goes on at home. Also, a child could be told "if you get too close to people they will hurt you or use you." These attitudes can be carried into adult life: A person needs to accept personal responsibility for the way they are, but childhood conditioning can leave its mark.

Fear of Deep and Meaningfuls: Others are afraid of confrontational issues and see "deep and meaningfuls" as something to be avoided. It is not what we say but how we say it that makes all the difference.

Having Something To Hide: People with a guilty conscience like to keep others at a distance in case secrets are revealed. For trust to be established a couple need to share events in their past which could be affecting the present.

Feeling Inadequate and Worthless: People who feel this way believe that no one really listens to them or cares about them, and that intimate encounters are a waste of time and only produce more pain and frustration.

People Who Hold Back Emotional Feelings: Emotions are locked away in water tight compartments which they do not want to be disturbed. They follow the ostrich complex and bury their head in the sand wishing to hide emotional expression.

Different Forms of Intimacy

Emotional Intimacy: This is where people express a range of positive and negative emotions. They become emotionally involved with a heart and brain reaction.

Physical Intimacy: Physical intimacy with family and friends has certain boundaries which are usually recognized. Sexual intimacy means different things to different people but usually refers to sexual intercourse.

Intellectual Intimacy: Couples who share thoughts and concerns about issues may take opposing view points but at the same time, they respect one another's opinions.

Aesthetic Intimacy: This is often achieved through love of music, art, interior design and cultural activities which can help enhance a relationship.

Recreational Intimacy: These people may play the same sport or be linked by a hobby or recreational activity. This could also be achieved through involvement with their children's activities.

Spiritual Intimacy: Some people have a belief in a "greater power" and find it brings strength and comfort.

Commitment Intimacy: This is a strong commitment to a relationship. Both people value the relationship and are committed to its growth.

Intimacy With Self: Being comfortable with one's self produces a greater sense of intimacy with others as there is a willingness for self-disclose. Intimacy with oneself is basic to all intimate encounters.

Warmth, Tenderness, Intimacy

To be able to obtain intimacy in a relationship which will result in closeness and honesty requires a lot of hard work. Some people are so afraid of openness, honesty and intimacy so they do everything to avoid it. Discuss the issue and show positive benefits that can be forthcoming.

Some people erect around them an invisible barrier so that people cannot get close to them. They could have been hurt in a previous relationship and therefore they have told themselves that this is not going to happen again so they erect a protective barrier. People, who do this, need to be made aware of what they are missing out on by building barriers. It takes courage to take the walls down but the rewards are enormous.

Intimacy is about creating positive, healthy, joyful relationships. It is about helping people break through their fears. Intimacy is about instilling hope and helping the relationship flourish.

Human Encounters of the Close Kind

All forms of intimacy are needed to maintain a healthy relationship. If there are too many deep discussions, the relationship can become problem centred. Close encounters also need to be enjoyable and playful for meaningful growth to take place.

Becoming Soul Mates Through Intimacy

A relationship becomes deeper when a couple recognises that they have a connection that transcends into the spiritual. When this happens they have a deep spiritual bond and are able to tune into one another on a meaningful level. To achieve the soul mate status there must be complete trust and honesty. Soul mates think similar thoughts as they are on the same wavelength. There is a special connection.

The Joy of Intimacy

The joy of knowing another human being on a deep, intimate level and of being known in return, is great. Accomplishing this can add meaning and zest to life.

However, achieving intimacy is not easy. The process is slow and gradual. If intimacy is achieved too speedily it is fragile and it can break down easily. On the other hand, an intimate relationship built upon a strong foundation of shared time, activities, and disclosures is difficult to destroy. The rewards of such relationships generously compensate for the time, effort and risks involved.

Case Study

Joe's Story

Joe was brought up in a strict religious sect. His mother and father instilled into Joe and his sister to tell no one what happened at home. Joe fell in love with Betty who was not a member of the sect and to his parents dismay he chose to leave.

When Joe went to counselling he had been married 15 months and Betty had become seriously depressed. He was doing well in his career as a project manager of a building firm. Betty told

Joe they both needed help. She told him she really did not know him.

Joe was asked how he felt about this and if it was true and he said that it was a stupid question. The question was repeated and he stated that he followed his mother's concept about keeping everything to himself. He had always been a private person and why should he change now as it had always worked. It was suggested there might be a better way — perhaps everything our parents told us was not right even if it worked for them.

Joe insisted that the problem was with Betty as it had occurred six months after the birth of their first child and he was sure that it was postnatal depression.

He discussed in depth how well they communicated. It soon became evident that their level of communication was at the superficial level. This was where Joe was comfortable. I suggested that Betty might come by herself for the next interview. Joe agreed to my suggestion.

From the first moment I met Betty she was open and frank and desperate to talk. Betty stated she loved Joe but the relationship was cold and empty. She said there was no closeness as Joe pushed her away. Sex was very unsatisfactory and romance died even before marriage. Betty wanted to ignite the spark again and fall in love with Joe.

At the next interview Joe started to look at what Betty needed in their relationship from an emotional feeling level. Joe struggled with these issues and decided he needed to talk to Betty.

Betty was now reaching out to Joe differently and he in turn was being more tender and loving. Joe was trying new skills at work and could see changes in the way staff responded. Life was rapidly changing for Betty and Joe. He relaxed more and even invited colleagues home for dinner and talked openly about what he thought and felt. He was no longer a private, guarded person.

Personal Reflections

1. Write down your personal thoughts about intimacy and how you see it expressed in your relationship.

   . . . .

   . . . .

   . . . .

2. Describe an area of intimacy you believe that could be improved in this relationship.

   . . . .

   . . . .

   . . . .

3. Comment on how intimacy is expressed in the following areas:

   (a) Intellectual Intimacy: . . . .

   . . . .

   (b) Playful (Recreational) Intimacy: . . . .

   . . . .

   (c) Emotional Intimacy: . . . .

   . . . .

   (d) Sexual Intimacy: . . . .

   . . . .

   (e) Commitment Intimacy: . . . .

   . . . .

   . . . .

Action Strategies

Let someone discover you – Intimacy means "into-me-see".

Let the universe give you a nudge – remove blocks. Learn to trust yourself and others.

Expand your thinking about intimacy – be committed to every aspect of life that produces togetherness.

Be open to self disclosure – stop pretending. Discuss changing needs.

Try risk-taking behaviour – do not always play life safe. Run calculated risks. Share your joy and share your fears.

Be prepared to explore all areas of intimacy – intellectual, recreational, spiritual, commitment etc.

STRATEGY 22

Let Us Talk About Love – Straight From The Heart

Love

Philosophers, scholars, theologians, gurus, poets and psychologists have been trying to define love since time immemorial. Their efforts, while interesting, have only some relevance to relationships because each experience of love is personal. For the benefit of this strategy the focus will be on romantic love.

Love is the most powerful force in the universe. If we could all only learn to love and trust one another, our world would be a far better place. Throughout your lifetime, your love goes through many changes. Each experience that comes your way has made an impact upon you. When your heart is open to love and understanding the impact of these crises help you to mellow and understand one another better.

Love can be expressed in thousands of different ways. Each person develops his or her own style of love. This often is discovered through trial and error. Hollywood and the media have helped to confuse sex with love.

Be Lovable

We are attracted to those who are kind and lovable. People the world over are crying out to be loved and accepted.

Love needs to be all expansive. It is a growing experience and you need to be willing to experiment in different ways to express love. Love can be in caring about another person, doing acts of kindness, or in seeking sexual fulfilment. Love is the oil which helps life to run more smoothly.

Falling In Love

People are attracted to one another for various reasons such as physical chemistry, personality, beauty, physique and other reasons. People do not really fall in love but they grow into love. As they gradually get to know one another there is a deeper expression of love based on intellectual, discernment and emotional feelings. Head and heart work together and there is an inner knowing that this relationship feels right.

Romantic Love

Romantic love can be fuelled by physical attraction, personality characteristics that appeal, and similar hopes and dreams that bring meaning to your life. You can become deeply involved through infatuation in the early days of a relationship. You believe at this time there is a possibility this is the right person for you. Unfortunately at times this does not always turn out to be the right person. There can be a number of romantic experiences before you meet the right person.

Three Most Powerful Words

"I love you" are the most powerful words in the English language. These words spoken from the heart bind people together in a strong bond. Love is not static but dynamic and will either mature or it will diminish through neglect. When the flame of excitement begins to flicker and eventually goes out, love dies.

When a person grows in love, there is a maturity in the relationship. Love is the connecting link that joins people together and opens them up to what life is all about. The words "I love you" are like a sacred pledge when expressed from the heart. In a healthy relationship the more love you express in words or deeds the more you receive back. For love to grow, there must be both giving and receiving. The ways to express love are limitless.

Making Love Blossom

To make love blossom you have to risk opening yourself up to the other person. You need to learn the art of balancing your dependency and independency. It is a narrow line and can only be explored through trial and error. Through questioning you are able to discern the level of involvement. It is a time for discussing your hopes and dreams for the relationship. Even in these discussions you cannot protect yourself from being hurt as you open yourself up, you are being vulnerable. You are revealing your true self and your needs. When this happens love often blossoms and the relationships enters a deeper level.

Kissing and Hugging

Kissing is a real art form. People kiss in different ways. A kiss can convey a thousand words. Kiss the way you would like to be kissed. Hugs help a person to feel loved and accepted. And produce a sense of closeness. To hug someone is to give something of yourself and your energy. A kiss often says far more when you kiss with your whole self.

Kissing requires skill, tenderness and knowledge. Too often it is only seen as a prelude to deeper sexual involvement. Kissing should be an expression of love from one to another. Kissing is not restricted to the mouth, but the hand, the neck, the feet, and other parts of the body. It is a way of nurturing and caring for yourself and others.

Do not allow fear or embarrassment get in the way you kiss. Experiment with the gentleness of kissing through to passionate expression. Kissing is an opportunity to share your self. What is so nice about kissing is that there are no rules. Kissing and hugging can be creative and is only limited by your imagination. Kissing expresses a message from the heart. Create moments that matter by giving the right signals through the way you kiss and hug.

Love is Communication

Responsible love needs expression. Love is communication. If one has needs of any kind, they need to be revealed so they could be acted upon. Even lovers are not mind readers.

You cannot assume people, even those close to you, will know and understand your needs. Love finds its own path, sets its own pace and travels in its own way once needs are identified. Share your needs with your partner as an act of trust.

Meaningful relationships do not happen by chance. Such relationships are built upon trust and honesty and cemented with the mortar of love. Love builds, love communicates. This type of love helps your partner to see the real you.

Love is Letting go of Fear

When you love more and fear less you discover a new sense of freedom. You let go of negative fearful thoughts and reach out to others with a positive sense of love and acceptance. Fear destroys a relationship but love builds.

Loving Yourself and Loving Others

Before you can fully love anyone you must first love yourself. Self love is quite different from self-centredness. Self love is learning to love yourself in spite of all your imperfections and to love and accept others who come into your life. Self love equates to self respect. Self love is the way you respect and love yourself. In recent times there has been much literature written on this subject by behavioural scientists who appear to be unanimous on understanding self love. Genuine love of self is accompanied by truthfulness and honesty. Such love of self helps you to see yourself as you really are, accepting both your strengths and your weaknesses. Self-centredness is selfish love that takes everything and gives little or nothing.

Believe you are the most important person in your world. If you do not know yourself, love yourself and care for yourself, you are not operating at your true potential. Discover who you were meant to be. Let go some self imposed labels that hold you back. Responsible love needs full expression. Do not run away with the thought you are not good enough. Treat others as your equal.

Love – What It Costs

Becoming a lover is an exciting adventure but there is a price to be paid. The price cannot be measured in dollars or in prestige or in influence. Love requires time, effort, communication, sensitivity and sometimes there is pain through simple misunderstanding.

Love is a willingness to give of oneself through touching, sharing, caressing and stroking. Love touches and fondles. It needs physical and emotional expression. Listed below are some suggestions to help strengthen a loving relationship:-

Time: There is no substitute for spending time with someone you love. This is not always possible because of work, illness or other reasons for extensive times apart. There can still be regular communication and expression of love during periods of separation.

Caring For One Another and Being Sensitive to Needs: Caring is love in action. It demonstrates your genuine concern for the needs of the other person. Be in tune with one another and recognize when your partner is anxious or worried. Listen to what is happening, ask questions, and be there for one another. Caring is showing acts of kindness freely and without expectation of reward.

Expressions of Love: Write a poem, a love letter or send a card to convey how you feel. Put thought into buying or making a gift, sending a card or flowers. Personalise your gift to make it memorable. Special gifts, as an expression of love can be given at any time. It is the thought behind the gift which reveals the depth of love.

Rethink Your Attitude To Love: Love is giving of your whole self, body, mind and spirit. Be willing to experiment with different ways to express love at different stages of your relationship. Love is fun, but too often we turn love into serious business. People are attracted to those who freely express love in unexpected ways.

Personal Reflections

1. Describe how you demonstrate your loving commitment in your relationship:

. . . .

. . . .

. . . .

. . . .

. . . .

. . . .

. . . .

2. Describe five practical things you do out of love to encourage relationship growth:

. . . .

. . . .

. . . .

. . . .

. . . .

. . . .

. . . .

3. How well do you express your love away from sexual activity? Rate yourself.

   0 1 2 3 4 5 6 7 8 9 10

Action Strategies

Believe love needs to be expressed. It is the "glue" that holds a relationship together.

Love requires thought, time and effort.

Little thoughtful surprises such as a small gift, card or flowers make a world of difference.

Do not take one another for granted; regularly say and mean the words "I love you".

Love keeps you in tune with one another and recognizes when support and sharing is needed.

Never let love and romance die in your relationship.

Love involves communication and honesty.

Put time and effort into your relationship.

STRATEGY 23

Love and Actions Go Together

Love Involves Household Management

Love must be backed up by action. Anyone can say "I love you" but the words need practical expression. You need to put yourself on the line and to demonstrate to your partner you mean what you say. You are able to show that you are a person of your word.

Love involves doing household chores and sharing responsibility for the smooth running of the household. In many cases in today's world both parties are working and household chores need to be equally divided. The same thought applies if the husband chooses the role of house husband.

It is all very well to be romantic and a great lover, but you need to keep your feet on the ground and realize the rubbish needs to be put out, the washing basket is full and needs attention, or to see that there is a stack of dishes in the sink. Love requires you to roll up your sleeves and be involved in the day to day tasks for the efficient management of your home.

Love makes you feel worthwhile and there is the desire to demonstrate to your partner how you value the relationship by sharing the workload.

Love Dies Unless Nourished and Expressed

Unless love is freely expressed in a relationship, aside from sexual desire, it will soon shrivel up and die. Loving words, thoughtful acts of kindness go a long way to keep love alive in a relationship. People need encouragement and support, and to be told on a regular basis that they are truly loved. When love dies, cracks start to become evident in the relationship and it soon falls apart.

Love Blends Two Philosophies

Love is the blending of two philosophies. Happy people who fall in love know what is right for them. They live by their individual or shared standards. They also acknowledge that the other person may have different values, opinions and ways of doing things.

In a relationship there is a blending of two philosophies whereby you can learn from one another which offers a solid basis for relationship growth.

Love Involves Risk Taking

Risk-taking! The sound of these words alone is enough to make you pause and think "There is a possibility I can be hurt". Life and love offer no guarantees and as we endure the pain of love it still can be a worthwhile learning experience. Taking a risk is central to everything in life. Without taking a risk, no one finds true meaning.

Even if we are deeply in love with someone, we can still hurt this person through thoughtless or selfish acts. It is those little things that we do that can make or break a relationship.

There is simply no way to avoid taking a risk. Continually playing it safe is childish, fearful and mistrusting of yourself and your partner. Your world shrinks and you become rigid and powerless. Your life has no clear direction. Love gives you courage to try. Even in our times of disappointment, the strong love bond helps us to heal and learn from each experience.

Real love often causes miracles to happen. When difficulties occur and things look so helpless life has a way to surprise you. Moments are often unexplainable. Love helps us to be in touch with ourselves and the world around us and to be open for the best life can offer. A thought, word or act of kindness may come into your life at an appropriate time and offer a solution to a current problem. It may appear to be God-sent.

We learn more from our failures than our successes. Some people even think they deserve what happens to them or that they caused it in some way or that it is the way things usually happen. This is nonsense; you cannot be responsible for someone else's rudeness, insensitivity, bad taste or cruelty. Value each experience as a learning experience. Keep the incident in its true perspective and stop investing others with the power to define you and what you need. You are not responsible for the action of others. Know if you need to leave a relationship because love has died and there is a lot of pain and frustration. Seek professional help when making a decision.

Values, Priorities and Beliefs

In any loving relationship your values, priorities and beliefs are important. From time to time these may change based upon new information. What is important to you may not be important to your partner. Be tolerant with them and out of love, respect their decision to change or not change.

The world is full of opportunists. Be aware you may be swept off your feet by some fast talking individual with a handsome body, sharp mind and well presented. You name it; the carnival of life can at times transport you into a make-believe world, and commonsense disappears. Be aware of this type of infatuation.

Live your life according to your values. Be prepared to value and respect your partner's priorities and beliefs. As the relationship proceeds adjustments will need to be made.

Hold true to what you believe has helped you in life's struggles. If you feel that you have to let everything go for love perhaps it is false love and not worth pursuing any further. Think carefully before compromising the standards you hold dear.

Love Holds Together the Fabric of Life

You have character traits, mannerisms, facial expressions, gestures, personality which are held together through the fabric of love. Remember there are only twelve basic notes in the musical scale, yet there are hundreds of thousands of unique and beautiful combinations that provide music for your enjoyment. Make sure you put together the right composition in life to bring lasting happiness. Know what you are searching for. If the loving fabric falls apart, your life can become cold, hard and a battleground for survival.

Being sensitive to the needs of others and responding before difficulties appear, is a sign of love. At times we become so involved in our own world that we fail to recognize the needs of others.

Love is Growth

Love is a growth experience. It expands your imagination and zest for living; it stirs your heart and soul. Doors that once were closed, open. Love makes you feel worthwhile as a person. It lifts your spirit and your view of yourself and motivates you to do something worthwhile with your life. Everything goes better when love becomes the motivating force for all our goals, hopes and dreams. Love is the driving force and helps you to put your best into whatever you do.

Love Is Not Manipulation

A loving relationship offers freedom from manipulation and allows you to be yourself. Think of your life like a block of marble or clay. You have tools provided by your education and acquired experience to shape your life the way you want to live. You have the freedom to be who you were meant to be.

Everyone has the freedom to express what they dislike about another person's behaviour. Once this has been stated then the other person has to decide if he or she will make any changes. True love accepts a person for who they are. The partner still can make positive suggestions which could enrich the relationship. Suggestions need to be openingly discussed. Loving is a harmonizing power which helps you to be at peace with yourself and those around you. It occurs through cooperation and not manipulation.

Love Is Like a Garden

Love is like a garden and requires tending. Unhealthy habits need to be weeded out. If you neglect looking after a relationship you face back-breaking restoration work. Leave it for too long and you will have to start all over again from scratch.

A well tended garden has healing energy that is obvious to those who visit it. It has colour and the landscape is ever changing. It brings joy to the hearts of those who carefully, lovingly and sometimes painfully nurture it.

Like a garden, developing a loving, fulfilling relationship requires time, attention and knowledge. It cannot be hurried. It is created in space and in time out of the substance of life itself. A garden attended with love is very noticeable.

Love Turns Ordinary Events into Something Special

With love you can make ordinary every day events into little celebrations and opportunities to express your love to your partner. Eat dinner by candle light; serve breakfast in bed. These little 'celebrations' need not be expensive, just meaningful. When love flows freely in a relationship, these acts of love produce intimacy and closeness. It is simply taking time to be with your partner while at the same time recognizing that each of you needs your own space from time to time. Recapture and renew romantic events that have brought you both pleasures in the past. Create activities that are fun and show how much you care. If there are children within the relationship, involve them sometimes, but other times make it a special time for the two of you. Adults need time to be alone without interruption and should not feel guilty in taking time out.

Personal Reflections

1. Think about your current relationship or a previous relationship when you fell in love. Describe what attracted you to this person.

   . . . .

   . . . .

   . . . .

2. Romantic love is a beautiful experience; it opens your heart and stirs your romantic passions. How is romantic love expressed by yourself/partner?

   Yourself:. . . . .

   . . . .

   Partner: . . . .

   . . . .

3. A relationship is like a garden and it requires tending. As you think of your relationship as a 'garden' describe what 'weeds' need to be removed.

   . . . .

   . . . .

   . . . .

4. Discuss any problem you feel that relates to shared household responsibilities. Do you believe your partner does his/her share of household tasks?

   . . . .

   . . . .

   . . . .

Action Strategies

Words and actions go together – love involves household chores

Experiment with different expressions of love – it shows how you value your relationship

Recognise your relationship needs time and honest communication

Keep the magic of love alive by thoughtful and caring acts of kindness

Strengthen the emotional connection by demonstrating your love by positive actions

STRATEGY 24

Romance - A Way Adults Play

The Pleasure Principle

The aim of the pleasure principle is to help you have a balanced approach to life, work and pleasure. Any of these can become all consuming and life lacks a balanced perspective. Pleasure is a state of mind. It is essentially an internal state but externals can add to one's enjoyment, the real ecstasy comes from within. Creating a pleasurable experience can do much to enrich a relationship. Play has all sorts of educational, physical, and psychological benefits.

All forms of life play; dolphins, monkeys, dogs and cats - all take time to play. They splash, chase, rough and tumble, tease and tickle. We love to watch their playfulness and can learn a lot from them.

Remember playful styles are individual styles. The way you play at being romantic should be right for you. Check to see how your partner feels. Be prepared to experiment with different forms of play and learn from one another.

It is important to take time to play. Intimate play such as going on a picnic, creating a joyful experience can do much to enrich a relationship. It is important to take time to play together and enjoy one another's company. At the same time it can be pleasurable to share these activities with other people that can enrich a relationship.

The human need to play and have fun is a powerful one. When we ignore it there is something missing in our lives. When we lose our playful tendencies we find our relationship lacks in joy, spontaneity, surprise. If this happens fun appears to have gone out of living.

Often, because of other commitments, people take life very seriously. The value of healthy play is often overlooked and perhaps this is one reason why many people are sick, tired, and unhappy - they have just forgotten how to play and have fun. Rediscovering playfulness can be an attempt to open up to a new form of expressive behaviour that offers a break from some of the pressures of life.

Life gets so demanding at times that we need to make time for play. Our energy level gets so low and you become lethargic and everything is an effort. Play can be a stroll in the park, enjoying a humorous movie, playing a board game, having fun sexually or simply enjoying a good belly laugh. All these activities can lift your energy level.

Basically We Are All Romantics

Within each person there is a romantic streak which is sometimes hidden because of shyness. Some people show romance more freely than others. Now it is time to discover the romantic that could be deeply buried within.

Finding the Romantic Within

Everyone gets stuck somewhere in a relationship. People who are shy can find being romantic very difficult. It is like learning any new skill, it needs time and practice as no two people are alike.

Romantics need to be creative and imaginative and for some this is not easy to achieve. It is time to experiment with different ways to express love. Browse through your bookstore and you will find a section on love and romance in the Self Help section. Be willing to learn new skills in romantic expression.

Learning about Romance

Be free to talk to your friends, especially those of the opposite sex, about romance. Listen to what they say and learn from their experiences. Some of this new-found knowledge will prove to be valuable. Keep your options open as you put into practice this knowledge.

Romance as Adult Play

Fun in relationships can be captured by seeing romance 'as a way adults play'. Learn to play as you share love and romance. Living a romantic life requires consistency of effort. Romance is an expression of love. It is not the same as love, but is the language of love.

Romance is absolutely necessary for most relationships. It is the icing on the cake. You do not have to be eloquent in order to be romantic, or write great poetry or love letters. All you need to do is to take time to look around and find the right card, book, or gift to share with your partner. Romance is not an end in itself. It is about enjoying life more fully - living passionately in partnership with your lover and trying romantic expressions to add spice and excitement.

Surprises are an integral part of a romantic lifestyle. Creativity and imagination needs to be built into your relationship - the essence of romance. The unasked for gift is the one most appreciated. The surprise gift is the most cherished. Think about when you last surprised your partner.

Romantic gestures have no ulterior motives. Their only purpose is to express love and appreciation and to show that there has been some thought and effort to express the romantic within.

Do Not be Afraid of Failure

Just because your romantic approach did not work with one person does not mean it will not work with another. Everyone is an individual in his or her own right and should be free to express their romantic self. Some are conservative and like to play it safe, and perhaps are embarrassed by the romantic approach. Try to put what happened in the past in its true perspective, and do not be too hard on yourself. Take time to reflect and think about how you could have acted differently. Discuss the matter with your partner and check out how they feel about the way romance is expressed.

Laughter is Good Medicine for the Soul

With the help of parents, authority figures and institutions, such as educational and organised religion, most of us learn to stifle or deny the childlike playfulness. When this vital part of us is not nurtured or allowed the freedom of expression, an unhealthy seriousness develops. Laughter is a release of the inner child and helps break this seriousness. It is a release of pent up energy when both parties are laughing and this indicates happy, fun moments.

Recognise Romantic Interludes

True romantic contact is hard to define, yet we all have a sense of knowing when another person is truly with us or off in another world. Closeness and romantic interludes occur when we are on the same wavelength and words are not necessarily spoken. This is a part of the magic of love.

Learn the Art of Flirting

Flirting can be fun if single, and helps you to become more confident in relationships. Flirting can be risk-taking behaviour. When you do it well, you will feel good about yourself. Be aware of the dangers if flirting gets out of control.

Hold one another's glance for a few seconds, but do not stare. In those few seconds, communicate "I would like to meet you" and learn to understand the response that comes back.

Be a Crazy Romantic

You may think of yourself as a crazy loving romantic. You know you need love and romance to survive in a relationship. For this to be achieved, you need to be brave enough early in a relationship to disclose this information. For some it may seem threatening, for others it could come as a challenge or to another it could be something that is welcome. You need to find where your partner stands on this matter. The response will indicate where the relationship is heading.

Rekindle Romantic Love

Perhaps at the moment you are feeling that romantic love has died in your relationship and it needs to be rekindled. The past and present live side by side in your mind. You can clearly remember romantic moments that lifted your relationship in the early days and assured you that there was someone special in your life. With the passing of time, romance may have disappeared as you have taken one another for granted.

The key to rekindling romantic love is the acknowledgement that it is missing and needs a concentrated effort by both parties to re-establish it. The way for this to happen is to discuss freely your emotional and loving needs that could add a new depth to your relationship. Remember the past, renew the present, and break out of a mould and let romance flow freely once again.

Let Us Get Romantic

Here are some romantic suggestions to help lift your relationship to a new level. Go through the list and try one or more of the suggestions. Romance is not gender specific. All romantic suggestions apply to both men and women. Remember, living a romantic life requires consistency of effort.

1. **Giving A Massage** - Expanding on the idea of touch, a massage can be a real expression of love. Study up on some basic massage strokes.

2. **Brushing the Hair** - Hair brushing can be soothing and loving. Some people love to have their hair brushed as this is very relaxing. Do not be shy or embarrassed to suggest this moving, romantic experience. Use candles and music to create the atmosphere.

3. **Foot Massage** - This can be very soothing and an incredibly intimate experience. Bathe feet in warm water, pat gently to dry and then massage with a special lotion or oil. Do not talk but enjoy the moment.

4. **Back Massage** - A back rub can be a way of expressing love.

5. **Picnic** - A well thought out picnic can be a loving romantic experience. Put thought into the picnic. Explore new picnic grounds. Make it a loving leisurely experience. Surprise your partner with special food. Read a romantic poem or demonstrate in some way that this is a special expression of love.

6. **Moonlight Beach Walk** - Sand between the toes, moonlight on the water, balmy night air can be a romantic experience long remembered. Tease a little, splash, relax and do something unusual. Consider "skinny dipping" even in your pool at home.

7. **Enjoy a Spa Or Bath Together** - Use music, candles, incense, wine and cheese. It all helps to produce a romantic encounter. The spa is a great place to communicate.

8. **Special Night or Weekend** - Planning does not destroy spontaneity - It creates opportunity - help things happen. For busy people planning is the key. Set aside an evening or weekend that is especially for you. Once in a while have a splurge and do something extravagant. Give this a lot of thought. Make dining out different - produce a card or inexpensive gift when coffee is served. Surprise your partner with a new location. Enjoy a bit of luxury once in a while. Design an invitation card inviting your partner to a special dinner.

9. **Enjoy A Dress Up Night At Home** – Dress up in your best clothes and have a nice candlelight dinner at home. Make it a night to remember.

Personal Reflections

1. Describe the way romance is expressed now in your relationship.

. . . .

. . . .

. . . .

. . . .

. . . .

2. If romance is the way adults play, describe some of your romantic, playful activities

. . . .

. . . .

. . . .

. . . .

. . . .

. . . .

3. In order to spice up your relationship, list three new things you would like to initiate.

. . . .

. . . .

. . . .

. . . .

. . . .

. . . .

Action Strategies

Recognise that it is time to rekindle romantic love. Even if it is good consider ways to improve romantic gestures.

Lighten up, play, and have fun.

Romance needs imagination, creativity and spontaneity.

Think of ways you could express romance – write a love letter, send a card, surprise yourself and your partner with a thoughtful gift.

Be prepared to rediscover the romantic in you.

Become aware of your own desirable qualities. Desirability is about building your self confidence and feeling good about yourself.

Be aware some romantic interludes will work well, and others may not be as succesful. Keep experimenting.

STRATEGY 25

Sensuality – Touch, Tenderness, Body Image

Sensuality As An Art Form

Sensuality allows you to express yourself, your beauty, your feelings, and your personal identity in a way that indicates to others that you are a special person. Like all powerful forces in the universe sensuality helps you to express your unique identity.

It helps you to have a greater understanding of body awareness through being in touch with taste, touch, seeing, feeling, and hearing. You have developed your sensory awareness in a way that reflects a radiance that is very evident in the way you present yourself and the way you relate. This is a depth of beauty that is within that helps you to be noticed through your loving gestures.

Sensuality has a power like seduction as the depth of beauty generated from inside flow freely outward to those you meet. There is a genuine love of self and love of others.

Sensory Experience and Sensual Loving

Seeking to understand sensuality adds another dimension to a loving relationship.

Touch: A touch can convey so much when you are in tune with one another. A touch can be a message of love or one of concern when touch is unwelcome. The sensory experience of touch can also be a form of therapeutic healing.

Taste: Through the sensual loving experience you get a taste of what is really happening in a relationship. It can be the nectar of love or the anger of disapproval. The taste of food and wine can make an event special.

See: When you are in tune you see one another with strengths and weaknesses. Take time to see and experience each new day and let some of those feelings rub off on you.

Hear: You hear what is being expressed verbally and nonverbally. You hear because you do not wish to miss a word of such a wonderful experience. Hear music, bird singing and let the beauty of nature speak to you.

Feel: You know through feeling how your partner is reacting and are able to comprehend the level of feeling acceptance. If the feeling is displeasing there will be resistance and distance but if pleasurable enjoy those fleeting moments.

Develop Your Individual Touching Style

Touching is a gift of the self. It is a universal language of love, whether you caress passionately or touch gently you are using the skin as a conductor of feelings. You are speaking without words. In time, touching becomes a way of life, central to all we do. Each person develops his own touching style.

Many of us have been taught, whether openly or by example, that touching is wrong and as such is something to be suspicious of and avoided. This kind of ingrained thinking is often responsible for the sexual dysfunction in adults. These constraints are difficult to shed, further inhibiting us from natural physical contact with others. Healthy touching is a way adults communicate without words.

Dr Ashley Montage, a renowned professor of both anatomy and anthropology stated "The skin is the largest of all our organ systems and perhaps next to the brain, the most important of all our organs". The skin has over five million nerve endings spread over the entire body. Touch can convey a message of love and caring. A body that is loved is listened to with respect and caring.

From the moment of birth our tactile sense is being stimulated - pushed, picked up, slapped on the bottom, and then placed on a mother's breast as the bonding process begins. This is truly a beautiful form of intimacy. From birth to death touch plays an important part in out lives. Touching is an act of love, a way of communicating in a special manner.

The need for bonding, a close physical contact with another human being remains with us throughout our lifetime. Some people express craving for warmth and affection, while others go to other extremes to avoid it. Much of how we function in the area of touch in our adult life depends on how we were nurtured during infancy and our understanding of the importance of touch.

Body Loving

Body loving is realising you are more than a body – you have feelings, emotions, attitude, and a distinctive personality. As you blend together these aspects your sensuality flows freely and your self esteem and self confidence helps you to have a positive approach to life and you see your body in a new light. Learn to enjoy your body and be proud of who you are. Your body may not be perfect but accept it for what it is. Your body image is not the same as your physical image. It is the way you perceive and experience your body, not necessarily how the world sees it.

You are not born out of a mould that came off an assembly line. You are unique. Your own brand of beauty is unique and has every right to be acknowledged and appreciated. The key to body loving must start with you and permeate every aspect of your life. The possibilities are limitless.

Touching and Stroking Out of the Bedroom

At times life is very busy caring for children, work responsibilities and household chores that there is little time for touching and loving. Often the only touching that takes place relates to the realm of the sexual. This needs to be addressed in a loving tender way. Touching and stroking in a non sexual way needs to be reintroduced to the relationship in simple ways such as holding hands.

Becoming Comfortable With Nudity

For progress to take place in your relationship you need to be comfortable with nudity. Let go of your hangups from the past. You may not have a perfect body but 99% of people in today's world think like this about their body. So you are not alone. Enjoy your body, have fun and accept "the droopy parts".

For many, early in the relationship nudity can be a tension producing situation. Set boundaries. Proceed slowly. Get feedback, encourage one another and be patient. Body shyness and inhibitions are major blocks to sensual and sexual enjoyment. Many people suppress their feelings and deny their needs and disown their bodies. Be open and honest in your discussions about how you really feel about your body image.

Enjoying a Pampering Experience

The power of touch helps you to reach out in new loving ways to enrich the relationship. Let your touch convey to your partner your love. It allows you to be imaginative and creative. Pamper one another. It could be through massage, brushing your partner's hair, giving a manicure or foot massage are some forms of pampering.

Little thoughtful acts of tenderness and caring indicate just how much people care for one another. It may simply be preparing a cup of coffee for your partner. Cuddling up to one another while watching television. An arm around the shoulder when the other person is feeling challenged by life's difficulties shows support. Simple acts of showing you care count.

Sensuality Enrichs Sexuality

Sensuality is a way to enrich lovemaking. It adds another dimension which focuses on the total body experience. It is a way to love the body you have and be comfortable with it. Through sensuality you come to appreciate yourself and what you have to offer to others. Believe you are a warm loving worthwhile person ready to take your relationship to a new level as you experience the importance of sensuality.

Sensuality, Body Image and Self Esteem

Body image is a product of our imagination. Each person can create a body image which reflects one's thinking about self image. If you can imagine it, you can live it. Train your imagination to be your ally. Imagine positive changes taking place in your body. Images are pictures, concepts, feelings, changes that you see taking place. Your imagination is a piece of psychological space where you can monitor the rumblings of the subconscious mind. It is also a theatre in which to rehearse new behavioural thinking and a way to learn to accept your body image as a means of overcoming sensual shyness. Being obsessed with your shortcomings, real or imagined drains you of energy which could better serve you as the fuel for creativity, productivity and self-realisation. Low self esteem keeps you from feeling the full impact of sensuality.

You become aware of yourself in the environment only through your body. The nervous system and sense organs transmit these perceptions to the brain as stimuli, and there they are registered in two ways: firstly as phenomenon, secondly as pleasant or unpleasant. Clearly an understanding of a person's body image will help in developing self-love and self-acceptance which will enhance touching, tenderness and sensuality.

Owning and Accepting the Body

In western society some people suffer from an inbuilt prejudice against the body, tending to think of it as of secondary importance to the mind. There is a tendency to think of having a body instead of being the body. But in reality we are one being - our bodies are ourselves. Our thoughts and feelings, joys and fears are all mirrored in our bodies. In today's society we have become appearance obsessed with the emphasis on how we look without accepting the total body package.

Freeing the Body – Stop Brooding

Learning to free the body is not easy. Our defences and inhibitions have become ingrained in our whole way of being from a lifetime of conditioning. It takes time as well as discipline and commitment to overcome this problem. The process of unblocking can be painful and confronting by reawakening old anger, hurts and fears. Without such strong defences you will naturally feel more vulnerable and sensitive. Sensuality can be a beautiful therapeutic loving and healing experience when you discover this truth.

You can find new role models for yourself through sensuality that opens you up to a new world. Be kind to yourself and be patient. It is extremely difficult to relate to others when you are locked into your worries and obsessions about your body. At times like these you miss genuine connection with others.

Sensual Touching – the Language of Love

For sensual touching to be effective there must be established a bond of trust. It must be agreed upon by both parties that what will take place is only sensual loving touch and there will be no sexual activity.

This helps the giver and receiver to know the rules. Rules can be broken if both parties are in agreeement. Create an atmosphere with candles, relaxing music and incense. Massage, a soft gentle loving massage can do much to rejuvenate the body. Massage is not about doing the right strokes. It is about being in tune with the receiver and seeking to provide a warm loving sensual environment.

Be adventurous as you develop your own set of rituals and sensuous experiences. Let go of any shyness and enjoy the experience. Both parties benefit from the experience. At times be serious and lost in the moment, other times have fun, laugh a lot and enjoy the spontaneity. Use your imagination and create some wonderful touching and healing experiences.

Remember touching and becoming sensually aware is an intentional act to improve every part of your relationship. Touching activities within the relationship promotes a new found freedom based on love and trust. Many people today, have a great craving for touch and tenderness but because of a shyness taboo have never fully been able to experience this sensation.

There is no limit to the variety of ways you can touch in order to demonstrate your loving feelings. You communicate your admiration and your affection by the way you touch. A little ingenuity and daring coupled with sensitivity and communication goes a long way to discovering what sensuality is all about.

Personal Reflections

1. Describe how you feel about your body image.

2. How important is pampering, touching, massage in your relationship?

3. Discuss how caring, touching and stroking is expressed away from the bedroom

Action Strategies

Believe sensuality is a way to enrich the sexual.

Be comfortable with your body image. Love all the parts.

Focus on what you like about your body and not what you dislike.

Become comfortable with the way you touch one another sensually and lovingly.

Be willing to experiment with new ways to express sensuality.

Be open to pampering experiences. Indicate what you like and also what is not as enjoyable..

Explore touch, tenderness and body exploration to deepen your relationship.

STRATEGY 26

Rethinking Sexuality – New Discoveries

Turning On To Sexuality

Everybody is sexual. Sexuality is an essential part of being human, the potential source of positive and joyful experiences throughout life. Yet a great many people do not understand their sexuality and lead lives which are not as sexually satisfying as they could be.

We are all sexual - young, old, married, single, with or without disability, sexually active or not. Learning about sex is a life long process. When you have an intimate relationship with another person, sex can be something you want to give and receive. It can be fun and playful, serious and passionate. It can be a tender reaching out or an intense compelling force – a type of lust, which takes over. Sex can open you to new levels of loving and knowing with someone you love and trust. Misused, it can bring much pain. Many people know much about sex and very little about love.

Sexuality is a unique combination of experiences, feelings, attitudes, beliefs and values put together by each individual. It is contained in "who I am", "what I am" – based on values and beliefs. It is about the desire to relate to the self and others.

As you change, your sexuality changes. It can get you into situations that delight you and others that you may even regret. It can be a source of vital energy.

Sexuality is very much an expression of you, all of you. If you have doubts about yourself, your attractiveness, or other people's reaction to you, these doubts can interfere with your sexual expression. Poor self esteem is a potential barrier to all aspects of relationships, not just sexual.

Unlearn Sexual Negativity

Many people feel negative about their physical/sexual self. Almost every person judges some part of their body - sometimes all of it - as not right, tries to hide it from view, feels ashamed of it even with friends or lovers. It's hard not to judge ourselves - and each other - on the acceptability of our bodies. The media has filled our minds with the type of body image that is desirable and acceptable in today's society. Talking with a body image consultant helps you to see that you can begin to think differently about your body and come to accept it more fully. It is a process you can begin at any point in your life and continue as long as you live. You learn more about sexual responsibility and responsiveness if you keep an open mind.

From my experience as a sex therapist I would like to offer my own definition of sexuality to stimulate your thinking. "Sexuality is love of self, love of others, and love of life. It is a way you express love, romance and sex. It is in the image you present, the emotions you show, the masculine/feminine in each of us. It is everything you put together in a positive way to enhance your life and to share with those you meet. It is life energy force based on self-love". Sexuality is a journey from birth to death.

Talking more openly about sex and sexuality with friends or in small groups is not always easy at first as shyness comes and goes, but we can learn from each other. At a personal level a discussion on sexuality can be fun, painful and healing as information is shared which causes you to rethink your attitude to sexuality. You can affirm each other's feelings, help each other challenge society's distortions of sexuality, encourage each other in your sexual adventures and learn together to be more assertive about your sexual needs and desires and find a sexual breakthrough which sheds new light on this vast subject. Make sure you share your sexual thoughts and experiences with a group of people you trust, respect and who will keep your confidence.

Your Most Important Sex Organ

Your most important sex organ is between your ears, not your legs. It is the brain. The ability to concentrate, to focus the mind on what is happening in the body, is universally agreed to be a major factor in sexual success of any kind. The power of concentration can enhance love making to an extraordinary extent. The ability is acquired through practice.

Love-making usually begins in the mind before the clothes come off and the physical act takes place. Your imagination plays a major role in creating what you think in your mind. This is why people can become so aroused by fantasy. The mind is a powerful tool that can work for or against you.

Do not be afraid to use your creativity in developing your sexuality. Prepare the environment, sensually, sensitively and with much thought. Take time to reflect on where you would like to make love. Think of the setting, use flowers, put a colourful light globe in your bedside lamp, use body massage oils, put candles about the room, and be free of interruptions. Create an atmosphere of peace and harmony by your presence and total involvement in the experience.

Prepare yourself for this experience by taking time to find more relaxation and peace in your own life. You cannot give to another what you do not have yourself. The realisation that you still have much untapped sexual potential is the first step of an exciting journey which can bring peace, love and lasting happiness as you share together. By sharing these thoughts it is a way to reduce sexual tension. Do not be discouraged if the progress is slow.

Our Sexuality is Unique Like Our Fingerprints

Sexuality is the most individualistic part of a person's life. It is up to each person to determine and then assume responsibility for his or her own sexuality. Many people do not take time to think through sexual issues because they are afraid of what they may discover. Be one of those people who take time to discover and develop their sexuality.

Sexuality as a Natural Expression of Living

Everyone has the right to have a good sex life as it is a natural expression of living. To experience a healthy and fulfilling sex life, we need to learn about and appreciate our bodies, know our feelings and our sexual responses, become sensitive to the physical and emotional needs of others and develop meaningful loving contact. The power of sex has a way to release our sexual energy which lifts our spirits and enriches all of life's experiences.

Sexuality as an Energy Force

Our sexuality is an expression of energy in our daily lives. At times we feel slow, sluggish, tired and everything is an effort. By turning on to yourself and your sexual energy there will be increased enthusiasm for living, reduced stress, improved self image, a freeing up of positive new meaning to life. Search for sexual knowledge with an open mind, focus on the positive aspects not the negative - be love controlled and not fear controlled.

Let Yourself Be Sexual

A part of being a good sex partner is being able to keep sex vital and interesting by discovering activities that can transform sexual enjoyment. Make a conscious decision to allow yourself to be sexual. Discover your sexual centre that turns you on to one another and to life.

The way a couple can turn on to their sexuality is by understanding that their sexual needs go through periods of change at different times in life's journey. This comes through honest sharing and personal realisation of what is needed. This honest sharing then produces a willingness to allow your partner to know when you are happy with your sexual activities or when something more is needed. A satisfying loving and sexual relationship needs time and energy. Like any other area of your life, the more attention you devote to it the more rewards you reap. Sexual activity changes from emphasis on performance to pleasuring as you get older.

Sexual activity demands more than physical and technical ability. Working through differences in needs and values can enrich a relationship and be a growth producing experience for both parties. Even before we learn to speak, we begin to accumulate behaviours which we discover to be acceptable or not. Our list of "do's" and "do nots" become an automatic part of us. Now is the time to re-examine this list as it applies to sexual behaviour.

A good sexual relationship comes through learned behaviour. Sex is a learning experience for both people. It takes a lot of practice, motivation, and a willingness to learn from one another and to free a person up to be their own sexual self. Letting oneself be sexual can be a liberating experience.

Reassessing Beliefs and Attitudes with Sensitivity

Personal beliefs and attitudes are formed throughout life. Our basic beliefs and values are often formed in childhood. Then as education progresses we are taught to question and re-examine these beliefs and attitudes in the light of personal needs. Each person's beliefs and attitudes should be respected and dealt with in a sensitive manner. Our intuition or our *gut* feelings will help to reinforce our feelings about our sexual beliefs. A person needs to be given a sense of validation to show your understanding of their personal belief system. A reassessment of sexual values can add a new dimension to sexual enjoyment.

Resistance to Attitude Modification

Some people say "I have been like this all my life why should I change now". This resistance to change could be based on fear of change. It could be that the person does not know how to change and is afraid to ask for help. It could be a deeply ingrained behaviour pattern to hide some deep seated pain, or lack of sexual knowledge. Any person can change anything about their personality, identity, ways of relating, and their expression of their sexual self if they are willing to work hard at it. It requires courage and persistence to gain positive benefits.

Assessing Sexuality

Human beings today have real choices about the way they will express their sexuality. The effect of the Victorian Era has gone forever and people in this more enlightened age are considering alternative ways to express their sexuality. They can choose to be heterosexual, homosexual, bisexual or celibate.

Making Adjustments

In re-examining your sexual beliefs and attitudes you can choose what is important to you and can make some adjustments without compromising your whole sexual belief system. Life is full of adjustments.

Time for Exploration

Positive sexuality helps people develop meaningful intimate loving contact in a sexual relationship. It helps a couple explore various modes of sexual expression from a positive viewpoint rather than a negative. The unknown and the unusual often produce a sense of fear and people often get bogged down in sexual negativity and are afraid to discuss sexual issues. Honest sexual exploration can help to improve other areas of your relationship.

Releasing Inner Feelings

In our search for understanding human sexuality the more we find out helps us to realise how much more there is to be discovered. Positive sexuality helps individuals to discuss sexual issues that are deeply buried within. It is a way to release these inner thoughts and to bring them out into the open and to share them with your partner. An intimate encounter takes place when both are willing to be known deeply and are able to express needs and dreams and are really honest about themselves and their sexual needs. This requires courage, integrity and maturity to face oneself and even can be at times frightening to convey this information.

Embracing Sexuality

A couple's sexual lifestyle is in the way they touch one another, how they communicate their needs, the type of sexual activities they enjoy and their general attitude to this important aspect of life. Some couples find it very difficult to articulate or even to consciously think about their sexuality. Some do not discover their potential for sexual intensity and deep intimacy until later in life. Others never discover their potential for sexual intensity as it is a subject that is never discussed. Whatever your age or stage in life, exploring your personal sexual style will do much to keep your relationship alive and it will make a real difference in everyday living. Be open to master some rich possibilities for sexual enjoyment. Even if you have a good sex life you can always improve it.

Case Study

Marie's Story

At 62 Marie never had a good sexual relationship. So she decided to get some help. Marie was determined to change but felt she could not do it alone.

She was the personal assistant to the managing director of a large company and had been divorced twice. Her two children were married and extremely happy. Marie confided in her best friend who quickly realised she could not help her. Marie said the reason she came for counselling was that she might overcome her sexual hang-ups and have a decent sexual relationship before she dies.

In both marriages sex was always on her terms, no talking, no experimentation, lights out and very little foreplay. She looked upon sex as something horrible and wanted to get it over and done with. Marie's mother told her as a child how horrible sex was. She had been bought up as a good Catholic girl and believed sex was only for procreation. Both husbands had tried to talk to her about the problem and she told them in no uncertain terms that she did not wish to discuss the matter. The main reason for the breakdown in both marriages was in communication and sexual involvement.

Now Marie believed she was never completely involved in the sex act and was thinking of something else. She never approached her partner for sex.

Through counselling Marie came to an understanding that sex affected all areas of life including her level of confidence, personal identity, and personal relationship as sex was life energy force based on self-love. It took awhile for Marie to accept the concept of self-love — loving self and loving others.

Marie had a real hang-up about her body and really disliked it intensely. She described that she felt trapped and when compared with others she felt she was a misfit. She did an exercise about what she liked and disliked about herself and only wanted to focus on the negative.

Marie could only say she was a good mother and grandmother. I explained that was a role more than a quality. Slowly she found three qualities she liked — (1) good with friendship (2) she liked her eyes, (3) she was now open to change.

As change was discussed Marie felt the first place to try was her hair style which she had for many years. The new hairstyle gave her a lift and she started to feel different. She received many compliments, and her attitude to herself began to change.

Marie began to relate differently and after attending an evening college course understood more about relationships. She read widely on the subject of love, romance and sex. She asked questions and found that both older and younger men were attracted to her.

Marie was wise enough not to race into a sexual relationship until she was ready. Then it all happened and she started having a wonderful time. Some sex was better than others. She was like a young teenager who had found something new. Life changed dramatically for this lady who had discovered her sexual appetite which had been suppressed all this time. She even looked 10 years younger. She was finding sex was something very beautiful and she was now enjoying something that she had disliked all her life.

Personal Reflections

1. Describe in detail how you feel about sexual enjoyment.

2. What do you believe you can do to improve your sex life?

Action Strategies

Sexuality is from birth to death – it keeps changing. Not all sex is good sex. You are never too old for sex.

Variety is the spice of life – learn to break the pattern of sexual predictability.

Learn to love the body you have – be comfortable with nudity. Be proud of who you are.

Beauty is in the eye of the beholder – how you feel about your body inside shows on the outside.

Sex can be beautiful with the right attitude – be honest face your inhibitions. Be free to say yes or no.

Stop running away from your sexuality – see sex and love as a key to longevity.

Section 4

SUCCESSFUL NEW BEGINNINGS

Give Life Everything You Have

It is Never Too Late To Change

Change and The New You

Graduation Day – Making A Fresh Start

STRATEGY 27

Give Life Everything You Have

Many of your thoughts from the past are outdated. From the previous strategies you recognise that it is necessary to change some thought patterns. Be prepared to give life everything you have to make a successful fresh start.

You are no longer clueless about changes you can make. There are many options that have already been pointed out to you. The more you put yourself into life the more you get out of it. Your life is what it is, not what it might become.

It is time to unearth some buried treasure that is within you. Celebrate all you have discovered about yourself, others and life. Learn how to attract the right people into your life.

Share your gifts, your talents, and your love in a new way. Amaze yourself and stop hiding. You have new social relating skills which will work wonders for you.

Live the new truth you now believe about yourself and others. Be your authentic self and let the richness of your personality flow freely to others around you when you leave the past behind.

You can now emerge as a delightful person with self esteem. If you feel some emotional discomfort it could be that something is not quite right. Life needs continual adjustments as nothing runs smoothly all the time.

Welcome Each New Day

Some days will be better than others. Welcome each new day as a new beginning. Each person needs to be acknowledged, loved and respected for whom he or she might be. You need to be valued for what you bring to life. Now is the time to get serious about life.

From time to time take a hard look at what you are doing and where you are going. Make sure that you are heading in the direction of your goals and dreams. Accept the fact that the best of life has not passed you by.

Believe more and more in yourself and it will show in the way you respond to life's challenges. In life it is not always easy to stay positive as it is often surprisingly unpleasant. In tough times, look for some positive outcomes. Your life matters so do not be deterred by set backs. You have new tools to cope with the temporary obstacle as you regain inner strength to find the best possible outcome.

Use your life wisely and learn from others. Watch how others face problems and learn from them. Realise you have everything you need to cope with life on a daily basis and that your beliefs shape your actions.

You are creating positive or negative thoughts daily and transmitting them to others. Begin each day with positive thoughts about yourself. You are the creator of your own experiences. Believe there is a powerful seed planted in your brain ready to germinate.

Know What You Want and Why You Want It

Spend time by reflecting, meditating or simply being still, and observe what is happening to you at this time. Decide if it is acceptable to you. Sometimes we get so busy doing, that we do not stop and ask "Is this what I really want?" From time to time your desires change and you need to be aware of this. When you are in the flow of life things seem to fall into place much easier.

If you feel you have lost touch with who you are, what you want, and why you want it you need to stop and catch up with yourself and reassess your life. Make sure you are using your time wisely.

Again, you may be feeling unfulfilled and you need to make adjustments in your life and lifestyle. Perhaps you are pushing yourself beyond your limits and need to stop.

Once you know what you want and why you want it, be decidedly courageous and do all you can to achieve your goals. Make sure that there is time to enjoy whatever you want. Do not let circumstances prevent you from enjoying the experience, either through busyness or any other reason. The desire to achieve arises out of something deep within you. Unwavering belief and absolute determination helps you to achieve your desires. Know what is within and waiting to come out.

Know what is important and let go the lesser things in life that do not matter. Make sure you increase your capacity to think intellectually, psychologically and improve your level of social acceptance. You can then become a better person and life becomes less of a battlefield. The desire to excel in life helps to override fear and self-doubt. If you can give everything to life, you will be surprised by the outcome. Your universe can shrink or expand depending on how you see life. You can make a worthwhile contribution or run away and hide.

Develop a new style of thinking that encourages you to put more of yourself into what you do. Break free from self-imposed limitations. Invent new ways of doing things and see the difference it makes in enjoying all that life offers.

Unlock Your Creativity

Be Passionate: As you make a fresh start, believe you are the producer and director of your life. A person who is truly alive ignites the fire of passion in themselves and in others. Aliveness, vitality and excitement deepens the bond and lifts a relationship to a new level. There is a good level of communication and the relationship is kept fresh and alive through passion, enthusiasm for living.

Believe The Best Is Yet To Be: Your life is about discovery, surprise and blazing a new trail. The way you see yourself determines the way you act. Believe life has prepared you for this moment. To advance you must stick your neck out. This is an innovative age. Unlock your creativity and expand your life so that it becomes more exciting.

Live Joyfully: Find pleasure in the present. Focus on what is uplifting. The present moment has a message for you. Life happens in this moment. Believe it can be joyfully dynamic. Make the best of life in spite of any difficulties you could be experiencing.

Your Life is your Creation: Be prepared to propel yourself into action. Change from a spectator to a participator. Do not let the past hold you back. Open your mind to new possibilities. Stand out from the crowd. Do things differently. Be an individual in your own right.

Keep a Fresh Vision: Keep dreaming, establish new goals. Know what drives you. Live your life like it matters – recognise an inner ache. Believe that you have something worthwhile to contribute to life. Be internally motivated. Really connect with others and show you care. Be focused and determined to succeed.

Life Changing Ideas for Relationship Enrichment

1. **Begin where you are**: Be prepared to think differently. Being creative and imaginative helps you to think and act differently. Take full responsibility for your action. Think outside the square.

2. **The Secret Connection**: This is a willingness to be motivated to produce some changes. Be experimental and make adjustments along the way. Patience and persistence pays off. The key is that you are trying something new. Turn limitations into opportunities.

3. **Keep The Magic Of Love Alive**: Whether you call it sexual chemistry or whatever, pay attention and express love. A relationship without love is empty and cracks soon appear in the relationship. Be fun to be with and laugh a lot.

4. **Listen To One another:** As you attempt to introduce the "WOW Factor" listen actively to your partner's reactions. Relationships take two to tango so encourage your partner to contribute with thoughts and ideas. Show respect by listening. Life is a compromise.

5. **Red & Green Signals**: The red signal is a sign to stop and reflect. It could be a danger sign that you have overstepped the mark. In life do not sweat the small stuff but on the real issues. The green signal could be an indication it is time for relationship growth. Decide together the next step to take. It is in these peak moments progress is made.

6. **Celebrate Your Relationship**: Anniversaries, your first date, birthdays all call for special celebrations. When you celebrate something with thought, preparation and the

surprise factor it shows how you value the relationship. Build in your own special rituals to lift a relationship to anew level. Do not be held back by thinking something is too outrageous or unusual.

7. **Never Lose Sight Of Goals and Dreams:** We have individual dreams and joint dreams for the relationship. Both are very important. Both parties need to be aware of the dreams. These give life and vitality to a relationship and take it out of the ordinary and make it special. Put thought and effort into what you do.

8. **Expect The Best:** Have a positive attitude towards the relationship and believe the words of Rudyard Kipling "The best is yet to be." However good the relationship is believe it could even be better. Anything is possible – work and believe it.

9. **Establish Foundations For Growth:** Know what works in your relationship and build upon it. A relationship never stands still as there is either growth or decay. Create your own opportunities for growth. Never be lazy and take one another for granted. Keep exploring and discovering more about one another each day.

10. **Demonstrate Your Commitment:** By your words and actions demonstrate how you are completely dedicated to one another. Be committed to do your best for one another. In crisis and in happy times you will give. Accept one another's differences.

Case Study

Lewis's Story

Lewis had reached rock bottom in his life. Everything he seemed to do would turn out to be disastrous. The night before he came to counselling Lewis was involved in a car accident, having driven through a red light.

He told a very sad tale. His marriage had broken up 12 months ago and his wife was seeking a divorce. He had three children and they all seem to blame him for the marriage break-up and they did not want to have much to do with him. In the last six months he had been drinking heavily and was facing a charge of drink driving.

Lewis now knew he was in serious trouble and this last incident caused him to seek help. He told me that his life was out of control and he needed help to get it back on track.

He was working in the building industry as a foreman carpenter. This was the only area where his life was stable. He was a very good tradesman and had a good relationship with his boss.

Lewis found a good lawyer to help him fight the drink-driving case. He saw the accident as a wake-up call as no one was hurt.

A friend he worked with invited him to go to church and meet some new people. Lewis said he was not a very religious person but felt he needed all the help he could get. Here he found a group of people who accepted him unconditionally. On the first night in church the Minister announced volunteers were needed for a working bee on the following Saturday at the church. Lewis volunteered to help. He thought it might prevent him from drinking. At the working bee one of the men invited him to a soccer match that afternoon.

Lewis explained how he felt about associating with a church group but he decided to attend church on a regular basis. He was not sure about the "God thing" but liked the people.

He was playing the victim role in life and through counselling started to see this clearly. He realised he needed to take personal responsibility for his actions. The church had a Divorce Recovery group and he joined it. After about six weeks his case came up before the court and he asked for a character reference which I supplied. His case was adjourned for two weeks as the judge asked for a detailed counselling report. He was fined $1000, his licence cancelled for 12 months and he was placed on a good behaviour bond.

Lewis decided to stop drinking and attend Alcoholics Anonymous. He used the money saved to help pay off his fine. He had changed his accommodation and was now living with a church family. A relationship had started with a young woman from the Divorce Recovery group. There was a remarkable difference in this man's attitude to life and to himself.

He was now making a fresh start in life as he had new tools to cope with the "ups and downs of life". He was reaching out to his children in a new way and was slowly changing in his attitude to himself and others.

Lewis needed to continue counselling as he had other issues he needed to deal with. He refers to himself as a "living miracle". He is well on the road to an exciting new life.

Personal Reflections

1. Reflect upon what you have to offer to life – gifts and talents?

    . . . .

    . . . .

    . . . .

    . . . .

    . . . .

    . . . .

2. What new truths are you learning about life and how can you apply them in daily living?

    . . . .

    . . . .

    . . . .

    . . . .

    . . . .

    . . . .

3. State clearly what you want from life and why you want it.

    . . . .

    . . . .

    . . . .

    . . . .

    . . . .

Action Strategies

You are responsible for the way you live. Give life everything you have.

Be free to be you – who you are meant to be. Know what you feel is right for you now.

Everything about you – your eyes, body, vocal tones are a form of communication.

Life is a series of moments – some better than others.

Courage is to act in spite of your fears. Think about your next step.

See each day as a new beginning – learn from the previous day.

Inner discontent is to help you to do something differently.

STRATEGY 28

It Is Never Too Late to Begin Again

It is never too late to claim the life you really want. Now is the time to begin again. Life has prepared you for this moment with new skills and new knowledge. You are putting the puzzle of life together with a clearer vision.

There could be a deep yearning to make a fresh start and to leave behind outdated thinking that has restricted your growth. Your mind is full of thoughts and ideas you are now ready to put into practice. You have some idea, though not always clear, what you can become. You are optimistic about your future and ready to move ahead with a new vision of where you want to go.

You know deep down a part of your life has ended and a new you is ready to emerge. For a long time you have been waiting for this moment and now it is here. Life has taught you much about yourself and at last you are ready to put these thoughts into action. Your eyes have been opened to see endless possibilities that stretch before you. As you dig deeper into your life you are now ready to establish healthy boundaries.

There is a spring in your step; a twinkle in your eye, your appearance on the outside reflects what is going on within. You are excited about your future and realise that you are ready for the next phase of your life. As you get older you come to realise that life is more precious and you are not prepared to sit around and let life pass you by. Believe you are ready to rewrite your life.

Your Past Is No Longer Holding You Back

It is time to let go of grudges and to move on to a new life. You have come to a clear realisation that regrets of the past no longer have a stranglehold on you. Holding onto the past allows the world to pass you by and possibilities and opportunities are missed. You are ready to forgive, forget, and move on. For those you have hurt along the way you are genuinely sorry. Perhaps you have tried to make amends which may or may not have been successful. Allow healing to take place in your heart.

It is time to say to yourself "How can I make the present different from the past"? You know at this stage of life you are breaking new ground. Instead of being fearful you have faith in yourself and know you will do your best as you face each challenge

You feel that deep within yourself "the best is yet to be". This is the message of hope that brings excitement as you approach life with positive anticipation. Resolve within yourself that whatever comes your way you will make the best of, as you are not wearing rose coloured glasses. Be in touch with reality and have your feet on the ground. Know in some way that you are different and feel an inner confidence to face each day and to make the best out of each situation. Your script for living is not one of limitation but one of freedom to embrace life.

You have new truths about yourself and this becomes the basis of your new life. As these truths emerge in your daily life you will act differently as you have nothing to prove but be your own authentic self.

Believe You Have Something Beautiful to Offer

You are no longer the same person as there is something beautiful emerging. There is softness and gentleness, as well as a firmness that welcomes people into your life. It is hard to describe but you radiate love and beauty that others admire. You take time to listen and encourage others. There is genuineness in the way you relate to others and there is no sense of manipulation. People are free to be themselves just as you are free to be yourself. You build bridges so people know that they can approach you with trust. They soon realise that you are a person in your own right and have the freedom to say "Yes" or "No" to any request. Do not feel guilty if there is a negative response.

There is no need to play the pretending game. Along life's journey there will be times when you need support. Never be afraid to ask others for help. This reveals to others that you are human and do not have all the answers.

See each person who comes into your life clearly for who they are. Do not judge them because they are not travelling on the same road as you. Accept the Buddhist teaching that "Every one who comes into your life is a teacher." Some are like a mirror and you see qualities in them which are a reflection of what is within you.

You have been given this period of life for a purpose to add new meaning so treat this as a sacred gift and use it wisely. Some people find life short and do not have this opportunity. Others are slow learners and keep repeating the same mistakes.

Enjoy this time in your life and do not be too serious - laugh at yourself. Be fun to be with. Share your wit and wisdom. Do some things that are out of character as it helps those around you to see the playful child that is within. Life needs a balance of work and play, doing and stillness and sadness and fun. Everything you experience is a reflection about what you are thinking.

As you begin life anew accept the opportunity to make your life really count in what you say and do. Slow down and recognise what you have missed. Know that something has ended and something new has begun. See your life come alive and be in harmony with yourself and the rest of the world.

Personal Reflections

1. What have you learned about life and about yourself?

2. If you could change three things about your life – what would they be?

3. What are five things you still want to do with your life?

Action Strategies

It is never too late to learn new things.

Have a reason for living. Be filled with passion and excitement at any age.

Consider what is possible. Be motivated by hope. Believe you have something worthwhile to give to life.

Become malleable, not rigid. Adopt a positive mindset to life.

Take time to discover your inner potential and share your discoveries. Make time count.

Open up your mind to exciting possibilities. Have eyes to see them.

Be young in heart and young in mind – keep learning.

STRATEGY 29

Change and the New You

As you enter a new phase of your life, know it will never be the same again. With new knowledge and new tools you are ready to explore a new life. Look closely and become aware of the changes that have already taken place.

You are ready to welcome and accept change and are no longer fearful of it. You see life from a new perspective and it becomes an adventure into the unknown. This excites and at the same time can scare you. You are aware that your future is determined by the present. It is how you cope now that gives you confidence to face the future.

Establish healthy boundaries that take you out of your comfort zone. Feel eager and have a sense of healthy discontent as you become a trail blazer and make new discoveries.

Do not wait for your life to begin. Begin now. Live in the now moment and recognise what life is teaching you. Clear away blockages that confuse issues, based upon past thinking, as they still show their ugly head every now and again. Know what works for you and let go of obsolete thinking. Be aware of what life is teaching you.

Welcome the new changes and accept the fact that they have transformed your life already. Remember the struggles you had accepting the initial concepts presented. Share these discoveries with friends as this is a form of reinforced learning. Not everyone will agree with you as there are still many who do not want to be disturbed. You are now ready for the next step of your growth journey.

Be Willing to Grow and Change

You know you are willing to grow as there is an inner urge which propels you forward in your search for meaning. Continue to challenge yourself and discover new truths. You are aware that crises and disappointments are necessary as well as the happy and joyous moments in moulding your character. Trust the unknown as life does not move in a straight line.

Believe the new you holds exciting possibilities. Use moments of inspiration as signposts along life's journey to keep you on the right track. Become aware of the possibilities of spirituality which could be God or some higher power, whatever it might be for you, that is available to help you find your place in this universe. Spirituality expands your life and does not restrict it. Love is an event of the soul and has spiritual qualities that lifts life to a higher plane and expands your thinking.

Spirituality and sexuality can lift your life to a new level. Sexuality is a life energy force that affects every area of your life including personality, identity, and self-esteem. These powerful forces can bless and transform your life. Explore these areas and recognise what changes you can make in understanding and accepting these concepts.

Genuine Change and Superficial Change

Genuine change helps you to take charge of your life and to make changes through patience, persistence and determination. Change is not easy because of bad habits we have developed. So to achieve a lasting change, effort and hard work is involved to overcome inactivity. This helps you to act more courageously. Once the pattern of change develops and you see results you know it is worth all the effort.

Superficial change happens when you try to please someone by your actions but your heart is not in what you do. There is no effort on your part to sustain the change. Superficial changes come about when a person looks for the short cuts to achieve their desires. These people talk about getting around to making some changes in their lives, but seldom follow through.

Change can bring about personal expansion and add a new dimension to your life. You perform better and accomplish more and create an optimal environment for growth. Genuine change helps you to take command of your life and broaden your horizons. It allows you to step out of your comfort zone, ready to leave your ruts and move forward.

Your life becomes your message and you become an agent of change. Life ceases to be stale when you readily accept change. When you plunge into change you feel a new surge of energy and become excited about where it may take you. When this happens you become aware that change can bring out the best in you.

Change, Creativity and the New You

Know it is time to reclaim your creative spirits. Be challenged as you explore this dimension of life. Put your heart and soul into the changes you want to make in your life. Change and creativity helps you stretch your mind and to put your life together in a way that will turn you into a stimulating and exciting person.

Let people see the real you – dance, cry, laugh, be a little crazy and do something childlike. Change is about having fun as well as changing serious issues. Perhaps you are far too serious and have become dull and boring. Change helps you to find happiness and your personality comes alive as you become more playful. Do something different that allows people to see the new you. Leisure activities should be creative, challenging, constructive and fun. As you embrace change in your social activities, have the fun of your life. See life as a creative playground full of joy and happiness. Rekindle your spirit for risk-taking and become lighter and brighter.

Personal Reflections

1. Describe three areas of change you have noticed in your life

   . . . .

   . . . .

   . . . .

   . . . .

   . . . .

   . . . .

2. How do you feel about your future? What areas still concern you?

   . . . .

   . . . .

   . . . .

   . . . .

   . . . .

   . . . .

3. What changes would you like to make in your lifestyle and your living environment?

   . . . .

   . . . .

   . . . .

   . . . .

   . . . .

Action Strategies

Patiently make progress. Ideas and dreams come when you are ready to act upon them.

It is not where you start that counts but where you end up.

Accept the challenge of change. Welcome it into your life. Be optimistic about your future.

Break free from the past. Feel liberated. Discover new options. Develop an "I can do it attitude".

Develop playful strategies for living. Live out your unexpressed side. Shine from within with joy and happiness.

Connect with people. Reinvent yourself. Follow your heart. Break free of self imposed labels that restrict you.

STRATEGY 30

Graduation Day – Making a Fresh Start

Congratulations

Having learnt a lot about yourself and life you now have 30 strategies to help you make a fresh start. You are prepared for this moment and have become a person of action —- someone who makes things happen.

The First Steps Are The Hardest

Once you get started there is no looking back. It's like watching a young child learning to walk as it falls down, then picks itself up and gets going again. This is true in your life. If you follow the strategies you will find life will be sweeter and kinder. You will see life differently as you have changed outdated belief systems and replaced them with new ones.

Accept The Fact There Will Be Difficulties

When learning new skills you could encounter some difficulties and challenges. See them for what they are with your newfound insights. Possibilities and probabilities are a way you can explore difficulties. Expand your thinking and creativity and look at a problem as you break it down to manageable parts.

Have Eyes to See, a Heart to Know as a New World Opens

A world opens enabling you to see new opportunities. Personal development enables you to grow and accomplish more than you ever dreamed possible.

You feel that you deserve success and become motivated in order to reach your potential. There is an urge to set goals and to believe you have a new ability and new talents to achieve these goals. A new day dawns as you awaken full of vigour and enthusiasm.

New Vision, New Confidence, New Skills

Move forward with a new version of who you are and what you have become. You have developed your self confidence, your social relating skills, and have a deep seated belief in yourself and are ready for this challenge.

Let Life Challenge and Encourage You

You have been given a life but it comes with no guarantees. It can be mysterious and unpredictable as well as exciting and challenging and can bring out the best or the worst in you. It is not what happens to you in life that really matters but how you react. Attitude is the key to life's fulfilment.

See Your Life and Your World Differently

See your world differently as you move forward; it is natural that you will feel some fear and trepidation. Believe you have renewed emotional resilience to help you bounce back from setbacks along the way. Look back and see where you have come from and what you have achieved.

Put Your New Skills into Practise - Be A Good Listener

You are equipped with skills which will help you to get more out of living. Life can be so different so continue learning new skills which will enrich your life.

Listen and be open to positive suggestions. Recognise that you do not have all the answers and are prepared to admit that there might be better ways to achieve your desired results. Admit when you are wrong.

At times there will be changes and modifications that will be needed as you move forward. These are perfectly natural as they are part of the human process of change and growth. Only you can open the door to your future and only you can shut it.

Know Your Needs, Know What You Have To Give

When you know your needs and are able to satisfy them you become more contented. Life needs a sense of balance between giving and receiving. Acknowledge your gifts and talents you have to share with others. It is often the little things that make the biggest impact e.g. remembering important dates, good listening ability or words of encouragement and support.

Strive for Excellence Not Perfection

Accept the fact that you will make mistakes which make a learning experience. Seek to improve the quality of your life and others by experimenting with different approaches. Be action oriented and believe life can be better than it is at present.

Start Each Day with Enthusiasm, Anticipation and Positive Expectations

To activate others, to get them to be enthusiastic, you must first be enthusiastic yourself. Make it a rule to let others know how much you appreciate them for who they are. Never let anyone feel you take them for granted.

Practise appreciation with a warm sincere smile. Your appearance talks to others. Let your enthusiasm for life shine through what you do and say. To gain respect of others, you must first think you deserve respect. Be an experimental person. Break from fixed routines and live differently.

Be excited and enthusiastic about the possibilities – be daring and determined. Every venture presents risks, problems and uncertainties. With your new skills you can approach each day with your new found confidence.

Limit your Risk - Limit your Life

Be passionate about who you are and what you can do. Be excited about what is happening to you as you set new goals and give yourself a pat on the back. Do not rely on others to encourage you. Be proud of what you are achieving. Set realistic, achievable goals.

Believe You Can Make A Difference

You can help build a better world by passing on the knowledge you have gained. A better world starts with you. You have a responsibility to make your world a better place for those who follow.

It takes a lot of courage to accept this challenge. This is an important moment in your life, feel inspired – and ready for an adventure.

Like What You Are Discovering

Believe you were born to succeed and recognise the limitless possibilities within you. To be able to share in all of life's opportunities you must exercise the power and the privilege of free choice. Realise that things do not always go as planned. You know you are a survivor, a solution seeker and you can be a winner in the game of life.

Enjoy Your Journey

Enjoy each moment of each day and fully appreciate your journey. Approach the future with heightened positive anticipation. Have a reason to get out of bed each day.

Accept Obstacles, Work Through Them

You have new skills to help you look at obstacles and to face them and work through them. Look for unexpected detours as the road to success is always under construction. You have new strategies for improving the quality of your life.

Living Your Personal Creed

Let life encourage you to feel secure. See your life as valuable and make it a sacred journey. Believe in your new personal creed.

Knowing You Are Ready To Move Forward

You are ready to move forward in your life and it is natural there will be some fear and apprehension. You are equipped with new skills to help you forge ahead. Believe this is an exciting time in your life and look for new opportunities to enrich your life.

Your Future Is In Your Hands

Your future is in your hands and you can make it what you want it to be. Be open to teachable moments that come your way. Be unstoppable. Be open to new and exciting learning experiences. See your life as a gift that has been given back to you. Use it wisely.

Aim for peak performance and do your best. Do not look for short cuts or quick fixes. Small steps in the right direction do make a difference. Believe you have what it takes to be successful.

Final Words of Encouragement

You have worked hard to get to this point in your life. A person is a product of his own thoughts. Practice the skills daily. Never, never give up. Have a winning attitude. You can be whatever you want to be and you have something special to give to the world. You are about to make a thrilling discovery as you venture forth. You will discover your untapped potential and find you do not have to do it alone. There are people willing to help you – all you need to do is ask. Have a ball and achieve your goals. It was Anais Nin who said "We do not see things as they are, we see them as we are." See your life differently and be ready to face each new challenge with courage and determination.

Self Evaluation Rating Scale No 3

Place a tick in the appropriate box as you evaluate your progress. Do not be too hard on yourself but be honest. Compare Self Evaluation Rating Scales No 1, 2 and 3.

Skills for Living	Very Good	Good	Some Improvement	No Improvement	General Comments
Self Confidence					
Self Assertiveness					
Problem Solving					
Social Skills					
Communication Level					
Listening Skills					
Decision Making					
Attitude to Change					
Positive Thinking					
Work Satisfaction					
Expressing Emotions					
Body Image					
Recreational Activity					
Expressing Love					
Happiness					
Purpose in Living					
Goal Setting					
Discipline in Learning					
Making New Friends					
Progress Evaluation					

Personal Reflections

1. What insights have you gained from reading this book?

   a). . . . .

   b). . . . .

   c). . . . .

   d). . . . .

   e). . . . .

2. Describe two areas in your life that you have noticed major changes.

   . . . .

   . . . .

   . . . .

   . . . .

   . . . .

   . . . .

3. Thoughts you have about your future – any real areas of concern

   . . . .

   . . . .

   . . . .

   . . . .

   . . . .

   . . . .

   . . . .

Action Strategies

Welcome to your new world – you build a reputation on what you do – not what you are going to do. Stop postponing your life.

Know what you want. You have the skills to achieve your dreams.

Self-awareness enriches your life – see your world through a new pair of eyes. Let the new you continue to evolve.

Enjoy your newfound freedom – be true to self and free to be adventurous. Be an experimenter with life. Enjoy your life, find true happiness.

Expect the best life has to offer. Achieve your potential.

Each day, see life as fresh and new. Live in the present moment and make the most of it.

Also Available from the Author

Beginner's Guide to Writing Your Life Story

A step by step guide to help you get started. Explore different approaches to life story writing. Included is a strategy for rough draft, basic English expression, and writing with humour, sensitivity and clarity. Price \$25 (incl. postage within Australia).

Oh Happy, Happy Days! – The New Rules of Retirement

This 276 page book is ideal for someone thinking about retirement or already retired. Chapters: Lifestyle Options, Living and Learning Skills, Search for Meaning, Single Living, Healthy Ageing, Better Relationships after 50 and much more.

Over 1550 proven concepts show you how to re-focus the young person within and shape your retirement as the best years of your life!

OH HAPPY, HAPPY DAYS!

The new rules of retirement

Live it, really, really live it!

GRAHAM L ASCOUGH

To purchase books or to contact Graham Ascough:

Phone: (02) 9634 4029
Mobile: 0413 363 947
Web: www.grahamascough.com
Email: ascough1@bigpond.com